Wild Creatures
of the
British Isles

(Previously entitled "Wild Creatures of our Countryside")

© Gwen Mandley
Published by Starfish Books Ltd.,
Starfish House, Brook Farm Road,
Cobham, Surrey
Printed in England by Cox & Wyman Ltd.,
London, Reading and Fakenham
Standard Book No. 900708 76 X
Second Impression, March 1975

Contents

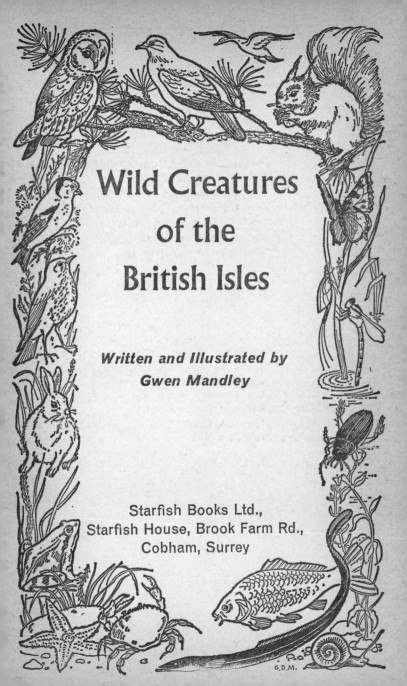

Wild Creatures
of the
British Isles

Written and Illustrated by
Gwen Mandley

Starfish Books Ltd.,
Starfish House, Brook Farm Rd.,
Cobham, Surrey

CONTENTS

THE RABBIT

Rabbits are sociable animals. A full grown rabbit is about 16 ins. long. Its back legs are longer than its front legs, It is grey-brown with a fluffy white tail, long ears and large eyes. Rabbits feed, mainly in early morning and evening, on grass and other vegetation. A female rabbit is called a doe. She may have 5 or 6 litters a year. The babies are born blind and naked: their eyes open when they are 10 days old.

THE HARE

The Hare is related to the rabbit, but has a longer body, long ears with black tips and long hind legs. Unlike the rabbit, it is a solitary creature.

1 The Brown Hare

This animal is about 24 ins. long. It is browner than the rabbit, with white underparts. Its tail is black on top and white underneath.

2 Blue or Mountain Hare

This Hare lives in the mountains of Scotland and Ireland. It is smaller and more rabbit-like than the Brown, with blue-grey fur and shorter ears. In winter it turns white for protection. It eats heather, grass and leaves of small trees.

8

THE BADGER

The Badger is clean and intelligent. It has a thick-set body, $2\frac{1}{2}$ to 3 ft. long, standing about 1 ft. at the shoulders. Its muzzle is snout-shaped, ears small, tail short. The hair on its back is coarse grey; its belly and feet are black. The white head has two black stripes over ears and eyes. A night hunter, it eats among other things, nuts, berries, insects, mice, frogs and baby rabbits.

Breeding Chamber of previous year

Exit

Tunnels

Entrance

Breeding Chamber

Sleeping Chamber

The Badger lives in woods, in 'sets' which have one entrance, several exits, ventilator shafts, and a special pit for refuse. Three to five cubs are born, blind, early in March.

G.D.M.

9

THE STOAT

(1) The Stoat is mainly a night animal – though you may see it in daylight – with a long slender body, about 14 ins. long including its tail. The head is small, legs short and claws sharp. In Summer the upper parts of the body are red-brown, under-parts are clearly marked white, tip of tail black. It is inquisitive and agile, and when disturbed will vanish, soon to appear again to investigate the disturbance. It hunts for food at dusk, and eats small animals and birds. It lives in both open and wooded country, and makes its home in underground burrows, where young stoats are born blind, in May to June.

(2) In Winter, in northern areas, the Stoat becomes pure white, except for the black tip of his tail. In the south this change is rare and a coat like the Summer one, but thicker, is more usual.

THE WEASEL

(3) The Weasel is like the Stoat but smaller – up to 9 ins. to 10 ins. long, and has a shorter tail with no black tip. Although a nocturnal animal it also hunts by day, often in packs of 6 or more, and its diet includes rats, mice, voles, frogs, small birds and chickens. Like the Stoat it can swim, and is very agile. It is red-brown with white underparts, but the division between brown and white is not so clearly marked as in the Stoat. The change to white in Winter is rare, and only in the north. You may see its nest of dry leaves and grass in a bank or hollow tree. The female often has two litters a year, usually of 5 babies who are born blind.

THE OTTER

The Otter is a very shy creature, not easy to see. It lives near water, by rivers, streams and lakes and on some remote coast-lines. It is about 4 ft. long and two-thirds of this length is its stout tail, used as a rudder. Its head is flat and there are broad webs between its clawed toes. Soft fur hides the ears and it has long whiskers on its upper lip. The coat is a thick, dark glossy brown, with lighter underparts, and whitish grey in front of its neck and at the sides of its head.

The Otter lives in a 'holt' – a hole in the bank near the water's edge. The living room is built above water level and has a ventilation shaft to ground level. The entrance is always under water.

The Otter eats fish, crayfish, frogs, water-rats and birds. The cubs are born in May, blind, but covered with downy fur.

THE POLE CAT

A woodland animal – probably now seen only in Wales, where it lives in open hillsides and sand dunes. It is about 2 ft. long with coarse dark brown body fur and blackish underparts. Its head has white markings near the muzzle and between the eyes. It sprays an evil-smelling fluid when attacked, and is very fierce. Its diet includes mice, rats, moles, frogs and snakes.

THE PINE MARTEN

Once a common woodland animal, but now very rare. It is nocturnal and a tree animal. The largest of the Weasel family, it is 30 ins. long, a rich red-brown, with an orange-yellow or creamy-white throat and breast, short legs, long bushy tail, round head and long whiskers. It feeds on small rodents and birds, berries and fruit, and lives in dense woods away from people. The young are born blind in March or April.

THE COYPU

The Coypu, really native to South America, is bred here for its fur. Many have escaped and are now established, mostly in East Anglia. A large animal, it lives beside water where it burrows into river banks, causing much damage. Its coat is dark blackish brown, with a soft greyish belly – the 'nutria' fur for which it is bred. It has large orange coloured incisor teeth.

THE WILD CAT

The Wild Cat is now only found in inaccessible wooded and open hill country of the Scottish Highlands, and sometimes in Wales. It is very different, being a native of Britain, from the domestic cat which probably came from Egypt. It is larger – about 2 ft. 9 ins. to 3 ft. long – and has a bushy, blunt-ended, black-tipped tail. It is nocturnal in its habits. The cat nests in rocks or a hollow tree, and 4 or 5 kittens are born blind.

THE FOX

The Fox is one of the largest and best known of British wild animals. It is very cunning, resourceful, active and quick, and a great nuisance to poultry and sheep farmers. Its coat is a deep red-brown with white underparts, and the front of its legs and the back of its ears are black. The white-tipped, long bushy tail is called a 'brush'. Including this tail the Fox is about 4 ft. long. You can hear its dog-like bark at night and in the early morning. The female, called a vixen, has a high-pitched harsh yelp. The fox hunts rabbits, chickens, lambs, all small animals and game birds, and eats fruit. Sometimes it is seen quite near towns, where it raids dust-bins and kills domestic cats.

The vixen produces a litter of cubs in March or April, born with woolly black fur. At six weeks they begin to grow the typical reddish colour coat, and in the Summer evenings can be seen playing outside their home, called an 'earth'.

THE SQUIRREL

You can see two kinds of squirrel in Britain – the Red Squirrel which is a native of this country – and the bigger and bolder Grey, which was introduced into England from America in about 1880. Both animals belong to the Rodent family, and feed on nuts and berries and other seeds. With their long curved and pointed claws, both are agile climbers and can leap from bough to bough at great speed.

1 The Red Squirrel

The Red Squirrel, now rarely seen in Southern England, can still be found in pine and fir woods of North and South West England, Scotland and Ireland, and occasionally in East Anglia. This attractive animal is about 18 ins. long, including its big feathery tail. The coat is red-brown, with white underneath, and, unlike the Grey, the Red Squirrel has long tufts to its ears. Its habit of storing nuts and food for the winter is well known. In spring and autumn it moults (changes its coat) and the winter coat is very soft and thick.

The squirrel builds a nest in the branches of trees and sometimes adapts the nests of crows or magpies. These nests are called 'dreys'. The baby squirrels are born in late spring and early summer; there are usually 3 to 4 babies in each litter. They are born blind and naked and stay with their parents until they themselves are adult.

2 The Grey Squirrel

The Grey Squirrel is bigger and sturdier than the Red, being about 20 ins. long. You are likely to see it in broad-leaved woodlands, parks and gardens, almost anywhere in England. Its coat is grey with a lighter underside, and sometimes in Summer it grows a rust-coloured streak on flanks and legs. This often makes people mistake it for the Red – but if you look at the ears, which are small and round and have no tufts, you will quickly see the difference. The habits of the Grey are similar to the Red – it eats the same food, is as good at climbing and leaping among trees – but spends more time on the ground, and can often be seen gathering the nuts under beech trees.

G.D.M.

17

THE SHREW

Shrews are among the smallest of our mammals. They are insect-eaters with flexible pointed snouts, long tails and very small ears. Their bead-like eyes have a short range of vision; and they have a musky smell which protects them from their enemies. Shrews eat a lot and can't go for long without food.

1 The Common Shrew

The Common Shrew's body is only about 3 ins. long, and its tail adds another $1\frac{1}{2}$ ins. The flexible snout is well supplied with whiskers. Its coat is soft, silky dark brown, with yellowish grey underparts, and the feet and tail are flesh-coloured. It lives in woods, grassland and moorland and in Winter may be seen in farm buildings. It is never found in Ireland.

2 The Pigmy Shrew

The smallest British mammal – the length of its head and body is $2\frac{1}{4}$ ins.; but its tail is longer, in proportion, than that of the Common Shrew. This shrew is found in Ireland.

3 The Water Shrew

The largest and plumpest of our Shrews, with a tail that is longer than the body. Its coat is dark grey-black with white sharply-defined underparts. Its eyes are blue and its feet have stiff hairs on the side to help in swimming.

THE MOLE

The Mole lives underground, so is rarely seen, but evidence of its busy life is visible on any lawn or meadow. It digs an extensive system of tunnels below ground level, pushing the surplus earth upwards to make molehills. The main thoroughfares run a long way under the turf – allowing the mole to rush from place to place. When hungry it must dig fresh tunnels in search of its vast diet of worms, snails, grubs and other insects. When exhausted it nests under an extra large molehill, called its 'fortress'. The mole is about 6 ins. long, with velvety black fur, a long flexible snout and small, hidden, sightless eyes. It has a keen sense of smell, useful when hunting worms, and very strong fore-paws, with stout digging claws and bare forward-facing palms. Every year it has one litter of two to six blind hairless, pink young.

THE HEDGEHOG

The Hedgehog is found almost everywhere in Britain, and unlike most other mammals is quite happy to live in suburban gardens – but its normal haunts are the edges of fields and woods, waste ground near to towns, and hedgerows and bramble thickets in the countryside.

The Hedgehog is a nocturnal animal, sleeping most of the day under heaps of twigs or in abandoned burrows. It is an insect eater. At night it hunts for mice, worms, snails and other insects, and will even eat young birds and eggs.

This attractive animal is from 8 ins.–10 ins. long, with a plump body and very short legs. The back and sides of its body are covered with spines about $\frac{3}{4}$ in. long. These spines are quite hard, brown with one dark and two light bands, and normally they lie flat against the body – but can be erected at once if the animal is alarmed or in danger. Its head and underside are covered with harsh fur of a dirty brown colour.

During the Winter the Hedgehog becomes completely inactive and goes to sleep in a bed of leaves and moss, in a hole in a bank or under a log. It will stay like this, without food or drink, for several months, tightly rolled up and protected from the cold and from its enemies. In the Spring it wakes up from time to time, and by April it decides to move to its Summer quarters and begin an active life. Sometimes you can hear one at dusk, snuffling loudly as it hunts for food among the bushes. Young hedgehogs are born between the end of June and the end of August. There are usually 4 or 5 in each litter, born blind, with soft spines, floppy ears, and a greyish pink in colour. At about 6 weeks old they are ready to leave the nest.

1 THE DORMOUSE

This little mouse-like creature is about $5\frac{1}{2}$ ins. long – smaller than a House-mouse – with yellow-red fur and white throat and feet. It has a long furry tail, large black eyes, and long whiskers. It is a nocturnal creature and builds nests of twigs and grass to sleep in during the day. Hibernates in the Winter months.

2 The Edible Dormouse

A much bigger grey-coloured animal, with white underparts, thick bushy tail and almost hairless ears. It is not native to Britain but was introduced into the Chilterns in about 1902. It sleeps by day and searches for nuts and other food during the night. It also hibernates in the Winter months.

MICE

Mice are some of the smallest of our mammals. There are 4 British species, the House-mouse (not illustrated), the Wood Mouse, the Yellow-Necked Mouse (not illustrated), and the Harvest Mouse. You will all have seen a House-mouse at some time – it is very like a Wood Mouse but has greyer fur.

3 The Field or Wood Mouse

The Wood Mouse is larger than the House-mouse – up to $3\frac{1}{2}$ ins. long in the body. It is brown above, with white underparts, and with a yellow spot on its chest, large ears and eyes. It lives in burrows in fields and hedgerows and in gardens, and is found everywhere in Britain. It stores its food of nuts, grain, fruit etc. underground. It does not hibernate, and survives well in the cold.

4 The Harvest Mouse

A tiny charming little creature, only about $2\frac{1}{2}$ ins. long, with an equally long tail, which it uses in climbing. Its upperparts are yellow-russet, underparts and feet are white. Its Summer nest is cleverly woven round tall stalks, lined with wool from willow catkins. You will see it in cornfields and reed-banks in the Summer. In Winter it lives in barns and granaries, where it stores its food of grain and small insects. It sleeps for long periods in cold weather but does not really hibernate.

VOLES

The Bank Vole

This agile little blunt-nosed mammal is found all over Britain, in woodland and hedgerows. Its body is about 3½ ins. long, brown-red with white underparts, and it has a very long tail. It eats insects, worms, seeds and roots – especially turnips. It does not hibernate.

The Short-tailed Vole

The most common of our voles. Like all voles it has a stumpy shape, with a blunt oval head, short round ears, reddish brown fur and a short stiff tail – all quite different features from the sharp-nosed mouse family. It has a greyish white underside. It is found in meadows and damp pastures where it makes extensive burrows, but its nest, made of grass, is usually above ground.

The Water Vole

This is the largest of the British voles – up to 8 ins. in length with a thick 4½ in. tail. Its colour varies from grey-brown to nearly black. It has a thick round head and small round ears. Feeds mainly on roots and vegetable matter, but it sometimes eats water insects, frogs, fish etc. Usually found near still or slow-moving water.

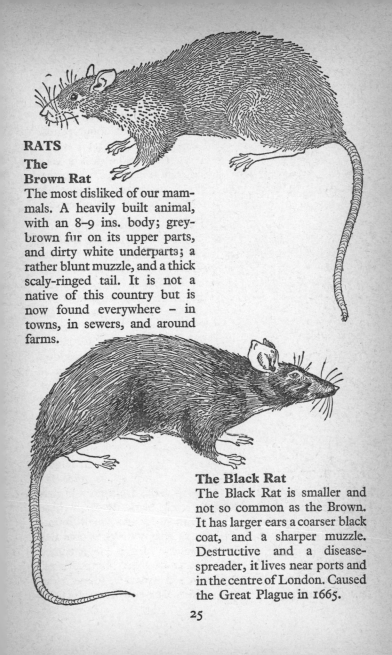

RATS

The Brown Rat

The most disliked of our mammals. A heavily built animal, with an 8–9 ins. body; grey-brown fur on its upper parts, and dirty white underparts; a rather blunt muzzle, and a thick scaly-ringed tail. It is not a native of this country but is now found everywhere – in towns, in sewers, and around farms.

The Black Rat

The Black Rat is smaller and not so common as the Brown. It has larger ears a coarser black coat, and a sharper muzzle. Destructive and a disease-spreader, it lives near ports and in the centre of London. Caused the Great Plague in 1665.

25

BATS

There are twelve species of Bat – the only surviving flying mammals – found in Britain. They are called Chiroptera, meaning 'wing-handed'. The four fingers of the 'hand' have been elongated so that they support a stretched web of skin, which connects with the side of the body, the hind legs as far as the ankle and nearly to the tip of the slim tail. This web gives the bat great powers of flight and enables it to change speed very rapidly – it also makes it very awkward on the ground. Bats are nocturnal and make shrill high squeaks, which they use as a kind of echo location when flying at night, enabling them to find their insect prey, and avoid collisions.

The Noctule Bat

The largest British bat. It has a round head and roundish ears. Its body is golden brown with dark grey, long, narrow wings. It starts to fly – a rapid zig-zag flight – before sunset. It lives in hollow trees and buildings, and hibernates in the winter.

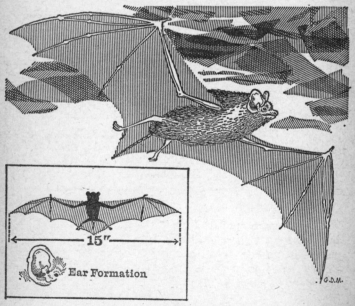

<--- 15" --->

Ear Formation

G.D.M.

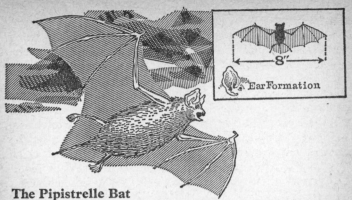

The Pipistrelle Bat

The smallest and commonest British bat. It has a flat broad head, blunt muzzle and wide mouth, and small, short, broad ears. Its fur is silky brown on the upperparts, lighter underneath. They like company, and sometimes hundreds are found hibernating together under roofs, in churches or barns.

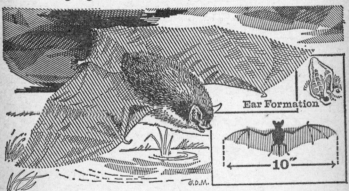

Daubenton's Bat

This bat, sometimes called the Water Bat, is found near lakes and rivers everywhere in Britain. It has reddish-brown upperparts. Its wings and ears are grey-brown, with a long spear-shaped bit in the middle. Likes company in Summer, but hibernates alone in Winter.

27

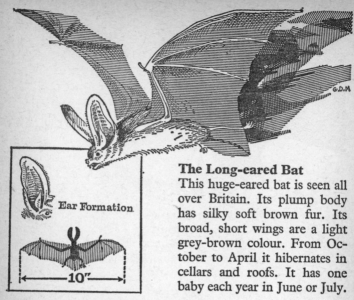

Ear Formation.

10"

The Long-eared Bat

This huge-eared bat is seen all over Britain. Its plump body has silky soft brown fur. Its broad, short wings are a light grey-brown colour. From October to April it hibernates in cellars and roofs. It has one baby each year in June or July.

Less common Bats which you may see

The Greater Horseshoe Bat

A leaf-nosed bat, about 4 ins. long in the body. Wing span of 12 ins. Grey-brown fur. Low, clumsy flight. Lives in caves, ruins, attics. Hibernates from October to March.

The Lesser Horseshoe Bat

Another leaf-nosed bat, about $2\frac{1}{2}$ ins. long in body. Wing span $9\frac{1}{2}$ ins. Fur grey-white. Pointed ears. Flies after dark. Has a low clumsy flight. Hibernates in Winter.

The Serotine Bat (Found in S. England.)

5 ins. long in body, wing span 12 ins. Upper parts smoky grey, underparts yellowish brown. Dark, almost black wings.

The Barbistrelle Bat

4 ins. long, dark brown body. Wing span 12 ins. Large broad ears. Not common in Britain.

The Whiskered Bat

England and Wales. Body 2 ins.; long silky greyish-white hair.

THE DEER FAMILY

Deer are antlered and hoofed animals. Three kinds are found in Britain – the Red Deer and the Roe Deer who are natives here, and the Fallow Deer probably brought here by the Romans. Only the males have antlers. These large branching horns are shed each year, and next year they grow again, a size larger.

The Red Deer

The largest British deer is found in the New Forest, Exmoor, the Lake District and the Scottish Highlands. The males, called stags, are 4 ft. high at the shoulder and have large spreading antlers, sometimes each carrying more than six points – an old stag may have as many as twenty points on each branch. The antlers are shed in February or March, and by July or August the new ones have grown. The Summer coat is reddish brown – in Winter it is darker. There is a white patch round the tail. The calves are white-spotted.

29

The Fallow Deer

This deer is smaller than the Red Deer, standing at 3 ft. at the shoulder. It is easily recognised by its flattened, palmate antlers. The colour of the coat varies, but is usually reddish yellow above spotted with white, with yellowish white underparts. There is a vertical white stripe on each side of its rump. In Richmond and Epping Forest a darker variety can be seen. The Fallow Deer lives in parks and woodlands all over Britain. Like the Red Deer, it is an enemy to foresters, eating the shoots of young trees and destroying the bark by rubbing it off with its antlers.

The Roe Deer

The smallest and prettiest native deer, about 2¼ ft. high at the shoulder. Now mostly found in Scotland; also a few in S. England, including The New Forest. The Roe Deer is a shy forest animal, nocturnal in its habits, only coming into the open to graze at dusk and dawn. Its Summer coat is bright red-brown, short and smooth. In Winter the coat becomes longer and a warm grey, the yellow patch on the hind quarters becoming white. Longer ears and shorter antlers than other deer. The Roe Deer keeps to family groups. The fawns, born in May or June have spotted coats.

Other Members of the Deer Family
that you may see

There are several kinds of deer that you may see in the countryside, that are not native to Britain, but which have escaped from parks and zoos. These deer have established themselves in woodlands and forests sometimes as long ago as 1870, and may be seen within 20 miles of London – in Epping Forest, Buckinghamshire, Bedfordshire, Hertfordshire, Hampshire and Shropshire.

The Chinese Muntjac Deer

This small Chinese deer is quite different from other species. It is only about 2 ft. high at the shoulder, with a bright red-brown coat which becomes olive brown in the winter. It does not live in herds, but in pairs or singly.

The Chinese Water Deer

Another small deer which originally escaped from Woburn Park, in Bedfordshire. It can now be seen in that area and in Hampshire or Shropshire. It has no antlers, but the male has long upper canine teeth which look like tusks. Its coat is a light chestnut colour with darker specks, its Winter coat is darker. In its natural home it lives in swamps, but in Britain it will be seen in woods or in reed-beds.

The Sika Deer

The Sika Deer is a larger animal, looking very like a small Red deer, except that its summer coat is spotted like the Fallow deer but is more reddish-brown in colour. Its rump is white, with a black border. These deer have escaped from deer-parks or have been deliberately released for hunting, and can be found in Scotland, Ireland, the New Forest, and in Ribblesdale on the borders of Lancashire and Yorkshire.

OUR AQUATIC MAMMALS

Mammals which live partly in water

Round the sea shores of Britain you may see two very different
kinds of marine mammal. There are two native members of the
Seal family; and many members of the Whale family most of
which are quite rare visitors. The Seals are highly adapted to
aquatic life but they must still come on land to breed; and
although their limbs are almost like fishes' fins and tails, they
spend much time on land on our rocky shores. The Whales
live entirely in the water, giving birth to their young and
suckling them under water. In fact they are completely help-
less on the land. Both animals are, however, mammals and
suckle their young; and breathe air at the surface of the water.

34

THE SEAL FAMILY

The Seals are streamlined long-bodied animals without a clear division between their head and body. Their hind legs are very short, the clawed 1st and 5th toes are long, and have a web of skin connecting them. Their fore-legs have been adapted to flippers which they use as supports as they waddle along on land on their bellies. They have no external ears and both ears and nostrils can be sealed when under water.

1 The Grey Seal

The Grey Seal is the largest of our two native seals. It lives on the West coast of Britain, the Farne Islands, Orkney and the Shetlands, where the coasts are rocky and there are caves and cliffs. The bulls sometimes grow to 8 ft. in length – the cows are much smaller. This seal has a long muzzle and a flat head. Its coat is grey, sometimes almost black with irregular brown or black spots. From September to October the pups are born in caves or on the open shore, where the mother returns for a short time to feed them. They are born with white fluffy coats, which they shed when they are about two weeks old.

2 The Common Seal

The Common Seal is a much smaller animal than the Grey. It has a shorter muzzle and a round head; with its V-shaped nostrils it looks like an attractive puppy. Its colour is a silvery or yellow grey with black spots. Unlike the Grey Seal it is found all round our coasts on sandy or shingle beaches and mud banks, in estuaries on the East coast, round the Wash and the coasts of Scotland and Ireland. Its breeding habits are different from those of the Grey seal – the pups are born in June or July, the mother coming ashore between tides for the birth, and the white-coated babies take to the water immediately afterwards. They very quickly acquire an adult coat.

35

THE WHALE FAMILY

Whales are warm-blooded air breathing sea mammals. Their young are born underwater where the mother suckles them. Their external ears and legs have disappeared and they are kept warm by a layer of fat under their skin called 'blubber'. There are two kinds of whale, the Whalebone and the Toothed, and the ones that you are most likely to see are the small Toothed whales with their single centrally placed nostril.

1 The Common Porpoise

This animal is small, measuring about 6 ft. in length. Black above and white underneath, it lives in groups called 'schools'. In Summer and Autumn you can see them jumping in and out of the water in the Channel and off the South and East coasts.

2 The Common Dolphin

This small whale, and the similar Bottle-nosed Dolphin (not illustrated) have been seen in the English Channel and off the West coast. The Bottle-nosed Dolphin, 12 ft. long, has a beak-like snout, and is dark grey with white underparts. The Common Dolphin (8 ft.), has dark and light bands on its side.

THE AMPHIBIANS AND REPTILES

Amphibians are cold-blooded vertebrates with bare moist skin and no scales. They are descended from fish ancestors, which, by a slow process of change, became the earliest land animals. Most amphibians begin active life as tadpoles, hatched from jelly-like eggs laid in water. These fish-like tadpoles breathe through gills and have a tail for swimming. As they develop, they change to lung breathing creatures with limbs.

In Britian there are only six amphibians – one native frog, two toads, and three newts. The two other frogs illustrated have been introduced from Europe – the Edible Frog set free in Cambridgeshire in 1837, and the Marsh Frog in the Romney Marshes as late as 1935.

Reptiles, too, are cold-blooded vertebrates, but their skins are covered with horny scales or plates, and they breathe with lungs. They are born from shell-covered eggs laid untended in most cases on land, and from birth they have to fend for themselves. The tails of most reptiles are used to aid movement.

Reptiles may be either snakes (legless) or lizards (four-legged). There are six different species of reptile in Britain.

THE COMMON FROG

The Common Frog is about $3\frac{1}{2}$ to 4 ins. long with moist skin. Its back legs, used for leaping and swimming, are long with dark brown bands; its fore legs are much shorter. Its colour varies from yellow to brown or almost black, and the patterns on its body vary too – but it always has a long dark patch behind each yellow eye.

Frogs hibernate in Winter and their eggs, or spawn, are laid in ponds or ditches, from March to April. In 3 weeks they hatch into $\frac{1}{4}$ in. long tadpoles and develop into frogs in three months. They live in damp, shady places, and feed on insects, worms and other invertebrates.

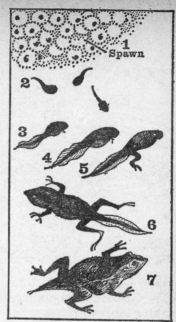

38

THE COMMON TOAD

The Common Toad is about 3 to 4½ ins. long in head and body with a flatter back and more solid build than the frog. Its dull warty skin varies in colour from yellow-brown to almost red, or a greyish-brown, according to the soil nearby, its sex or its age. The elongated swelling behind its eye is its parotid gland. The front legs are short, thick and powerful, and the toes of its hind legs are webbed. The Toad shelters by day under stones or tree roots and comes out at night to hunt for food. It eats worms, snails, caterpillars and even small mice.

Like the frog, it hibernates during the Winter months, re-appearing in late March. Eggs are laid, in double-rowed strings, in April, and in 8–10 days the very small tadpoles emerge. The tadpole becomes a small active toad, about ⅓ in. long, by the end of June. Fully grown after 4 years.

Toad Spawn

The Marsh Frog

Our largest frog, up to 6¾ ins. long, has a warty moist skin, olive-green with greyish-white underparts. Found only on Romney Marsh. It has a loud laughing croak at breeding times in April and May.

The Edible Frog

Another green frog, smaller (4 ins. long) with skin blotched with black, a pale green line down its back and yellow-white underparts. It has short legs, and its hind leg toes are long and webbed.

The Natterjack Toad

Smaller, (about 3 ins. long) and shorter-legged than the Common Toad, warty skin, grey olive-green or brownish with yellow line down its back. Found dry sandy places. Rare.

THE NEWTS

There are three British species of newts. They are slender animals with small heads and long, broad, paddle-like tails. The four limbs are equal in length. The front legs have four toes, the back legs five. Newts begin life as jelly-covered eggs, laid singly on a leaf of pond-weed. In two weeks the eggs hatch into slim tadpoles breathing by gills. Eventually the gills become lungs and the newt becomes a land animal.

1 The Crested Newt
Dark brown black-speckled newt, with black-spotted orange belly. In the mating season the male grows a crest on its back.

5″– 7″ long

female ①

2 The Smooth Newt
The most common newt, its back olive, spotted black; middle parts yellow or orange; flanks whitish with black spots. At the breeding time males are crested.

3 The Palmate Newt
The smallest British newt. Slender, with smooth olive-green skin marked darker green, and pale orange-yellow on its underside.

2¾″– 3½″ long

② female

③ female

3″ long.

41

THE LIZARDS

There are only 3 species of lizard in the British Isles. The Common Lizard is seen in all parts of the country, but the Sand Lizard is only found in Southern England. The third lizard, the snake-like Slow Worm, doesn't look like one at all, but it has the movable eye-lids and fixed jaw-bone common to all lizards. Lizards, like snakes, have horny scales.

1 The Common Lizard

A slender lizard, 4 to $6\frac{1}{4}$ ins. long. Its brown back has dark stripes down the middle and sides. The male's underparts are yellow-red, black spotted. Likes damp moors and woodland.

2 The Sand Lizard

A large lizard, 8 ins. long. Its colour varies, but the upperparts are usually brown with darker rings and white 'eye' spots along its sides. In Spring the male is green.

3 The Slow Worm

A reptile with a long, legless, smooth-scaled body. Blue-grey above with a black belly.

THE SNAKES

Of the 3 British snakes, the Grass Snake is common except in Ireland and Scotland; the Adder is fairly common and also venomous, so beware and leave it alone. The Smooth Snake is very rare. Snakes have long bodies, short tails and no limbs. The body is covered with horny scales; jaws are loosely joined and their tongues are forked.

1 The Grass Snake

A slender creature, about 2½ ft. long. Grey-brown with small dark markings on the side of the body. Two crescent shapes, bordered in black behind its head.

2 The Adder or Viper

A short thick snake, 18 ins. long, heavily marked with zigzags, black on varying grounds from white to dark brown, with a V-shaped mark on its head.

3 The Smooth Snake

Has a soft body with smooth scales. It is 2 ft. long, coloured purple-grey, with broken blackish markings and a brown head.

G.D.M.

43

BIRDS

There are 336 different species of bird to be found in our countryside.* Of these 131 are said to be 'residents', 54 are 'Summer visitors' coming here to breed and bring up their young; 26 are 'Winter visitors', often on their way to warmer climates; 23 are 'occasional visitors'; and 100 are classed as 'rare'. There is one, the Great Auk, which is now extinct.

Here we have only room to show you the residents, the Summer visitors, and a few well-known Winter visitors. As the birds vary so much in size it has been impossible to illustrate them on the same scale, so the approximate length of each bird is given in inches, measured from the tip of its bill to the tip of its longest tail feather. We have also described the colour of each bird, and the kind of country where you may see it.

All these birds are our heritage. We must do all that we can to protect them: enjoy watching them, but never do anything that harms or destroys them.

* *From the list of British Birds published by the Ornithological Society, in 1941, and re-issued in 1960.*

THE CROWS

The Crows are all large birds with heavy bills and rounded wings. They have harsh voices and are disliked by other birds.

The Raven

The Raven is the largest and most powerful of the crow family, and is now common only in remote and undisturbed areas. It is about 25 ins. from its decidedly hooked beak to its tail, with black legs, feet and beak, and glossy plumage. It is usually seen singly or in pairs. It has a very hoarse deep croak.

The Hooded Crow

Smaller than the Raven – 18 ins. long – the Hooded Crow has black plumage on its head, throat, wings, and tail, but is ash-grey everywhere else. It has a black bill and black legs and dark brown eyes. Common in open country, it is also seen in cities, where it mixes and sometimes breeds with the Carrion Crow.

The Carrion Crow

This bird looks and behaves very like the Raven, but is smaller (18–20 ins.), has a shorter, less curved beak and a square tail. A solitary bird, it nests in pairs in trees or on cliffs. Its plumage is black, with a green sheen and its legs and bill are also black.

45

The Rook
It nests in 'rookeries', often near houses, and feeds in flocks in open fields. At evening you can see these flocks returning to roost. 18 ins. long, it has glossy black plumage with a pale area at the base of its bill.

The Jackdaw
A much smaller bird than the Rook – only 13 ins. long.

Sociable, with perky movements, glossy black on head and upper wings, duller black beneath, with grey nape of neck and sides of face. Has a short straight beak and white or pale blue eyes. Gives a shrill 'tchack'.

The Chough
Sadly, this is becoming a rare bird, seen only on high mountains and rocky coasts. It is 15 ins. long, and has glossy blue-black plumage with a green sheen on its wings and a square tail. Its long, curved, coral-coloured beak and legs easily distinguish it from other crows.

The Starling
A friendly bird, 8½ ins. long with metallic speckled plumage, short tail and long yellow bill. It likes to be near human habitation and feeds in gardens, pastures and ploughed land. At dusk flocks congregate in large roosts, especially in towns.

1 The Magpie

A member of the Crow family, the Magpie is a very common bird. Usually seen in pairs, its glossy black and white plumage and very long tail are easily recognised. It is 18 ins. long with a 9 in. tail.

It loves bright objects and is known as a thief. Some people think that it is unlucky to see only one bird and there is a saying 'One for sorrow, two for joy'.

2 The Jay

Also one of the Crow family. A woodland bird, 14 ins. long, with a white, black-streaked crest; a pinky grey head, back and breast; with pure white chin, throat, belly and base of tail. Its tail is brownish black, and its wings black, white, and chestnut with beautiful black, white and bright blue barred feathers on the side wings.

47

1 The Bullfinch

A handsome finch, to be seen in woods, parks and gardens, if you watch carefully. It is a quite common bird, but very shy. Its habit of eating fruit buds makes it unpopular with gardeners. It is about 5¾ ins. long. The male's head, chin, tail and wings are glossy black. The wings have a white bar, and his rump is white. His back is blue-grey and his cheeks and underparts are a brick red. The female is a more subdued colour.

2 The Linnet

A sociable bird, 5 ins. long, often seen with other finches, on heaths and in open country, marshes and sandhills. It feeds on seeds, and has a pleasant twittering song. The male has a chestnut brown back, with fawn to white underparts. His head is greyish-brown with darker streaks and he has a beautiful crimson forehead, crown and breast. His flight feathers and forked tail have white edges. The colour of the female is duller with no red patches.

3 The Twite

Very like the Linnet, but without the red head and breast, the Twite is found on moorlands and mountains. It has a yellow bill, and in Scotland is called the 'Yellow-neb Lintie'. The striped plumage of the male is pale reddish brown, with a pinkish rump. It has white patches on wings and tail. The female is similar, but has a greyish-brown rump. It is 5¼ ins. long.

4 The Crossbill

Mostly seen in Scotland, in the coniferous forests. A large stumpy, short-necked bird, 6½ ins. long, easily recognised by its curious crossed bill. The male has distinctive red plumage. The female is green. It feeds on fir-cone seeds and can be watched climbing along fir branches like an acrobat, or a parrot, tearing at the cones to get at the seeds.

51

G.D.M.

The Chaffinch

The Chaffinch is one of our most familiar birds, and can be
seen everywhere in the British Isles, in woods, gardens and
parks. It has a cheerful call, sung by both males and females,
which sounds like 'pink pink'. It is heard at all times of the
year, but in Spring the male has a lilting song, sometimes
ending with a harsh rattle.

It feeds on seeds, and in Spring and Summer, on insects. It
is about 6 ins. long. The head of the male is slate-blue on the
crown and the nape, but with pinkish chestnut cheeks. His
back is warm chestnut colour with a greenish rump, his breast
is deep pink shading to white. He has distinct white wing bars
and white on his outer tail feathers. The female is yellowish-
brown above, greenish on the rump and pale underneath.

THE BUNTINGS The Buntings have short, thick bills and large heads. Sparrow-sized, they nest in low bushes or on the ground. They eat seeds.

1 The Corn Bunting Common in open country, where it likes an exposed perch from which to sing. Both sexes have grey-brown plumage streaked with dark brown.

2 The Yellowhammer Found in open country, where its song 'a little bit of bread and no cheese' is heard from February to September. 6½ ins. long with a yellow head, throat and underparts, chestnut back and flanks, brown-streaked.

3 Cirl Bunting Like the Yellow Hammer, but with black chin, throat and stripe through eye. Yellow breast with olive band, upper-parts olive brown. 6½ ins. long. A tree-frequenting species.

4 Reed Bunting Lives among reeds. The male has a black head and throat with white collar. He is 6 ins. long with brown, dark streaked upper-parts and white under-parts and outer tail feathers.

5 The Snow Bunting Common in the Scottish Highlands and high treeless parts of Britain. 6½ ins. long, the male is a black and white, the female brown and white.

53

G.D.M.

WEAVER FINCHES
Small, thick-billed, short-legged birds. Sociable, they feed on the ground and make nests in holes, or build domed nests.

1 The House Sparrow
Seen everywhere, on farms, in towns and villages, liking to live near man. The male bird is $5\frac{3}{4}$ ins. long, with a grey crown, black throat, and brown-streaked back. The female has no black on head or throat. It nests under roofs, in holes or builds bulky domed nests in bushes and trees.

2 The Tree Sparrow
Smaller and more slender than the House Sparrow. $5\frac{1}{2}$ ins. long. The male has a chestnut crown, much smaller black bib, and a black spot on his white cheek. The female is similar. It nests in trees away from houses.

THE LARKS

Small or medium-sized birds of the open country, who sing while flying, beginning their song when a few feet from the ground. Nest on the ground.

1 The Skylark

A brown bird, 7 ins. long, with streaked head, back and flanks, and a noticeable pale buff eye stripe. It has a small crest and a long, white-edged tail. The open country is its home.

2 The Woodlark

Found in clearings and woods, on heaths and mountains, it resembles the Skylark but is smaller – 6 ins. long – and has a shorter tail. It perches on trees or bushes; often sings at night.

THE PIPPITS AND WAGTAILS

These sparrow-sized birds have dark tails with white outer feathers and slender bills. They walk instead of hopping, and their tails wag continually.

The Rock Pippit

A coast loving bird, never far from rocks, 6½ ins. long with dark olive-brown plumage, sandy-buff spotted underparts, and smoky grey tail feathers. Its legs are dark coloured.

1 The Grey Wagtail

This bird is found near running water, especially mountain streams. It is 7 ins. long, has a yellow underside, slate-coloured head and back, and black long tail. In the Summer the male bird has a black throat. Slim and graceful, you will see it flitting from stone to stone, its tail dipping up and down. Feeds on insects. Found in the winter by sewage farms and lakes.

2 The Pied Wagtail

Another water bird, found on river and stream banks, and lake edges. 7 ins. long, it has a solid black back, white tips to its wing feathers, a black tail with white outer feathers, and a black throat. It nests in stream banks, and feeds on insects, sometimes catching them in the air.

The Tree Pippit (*not illustrated*)

Like all Pippits, this bird walks, and does not hop. It is 6 ins. long, light brown coloured, streaked with dark brown.

The Meadow Pippit (*not illustrated*)

A very common uplands bird, 6 ins. long, with brown-streaked plumage, whiter on the breast than the Tree Pippit.

The Yellow Wagtail (*not illustrated*)

A Summer visitor to open country, meadows and commons.

THE NUTHATCH

A stocky bird, 5½ ins. long, with a strong pointed beak, short tail and legs, and sharp curved claws. It is common in old woods and parkland in Southern England. It has grey-blue upperparts, buff underparts and chestnut flanks, white cheeks and throat, and a black stripe through its eye. It climbs up and down trunks of trees with jerky movements, using its beak like a hammer.

THE TREECREEPER

This bird is found everywhere in Britain, in woods, gardens and open country, but there are not many of them. It is smaller than a sparrow, about 5 ins. long, with grey-brown streaked upper parts, and white under-parts. It has a stiff pointed tail, a curved bill, and large feet. It creeps spirally up trees in its search for insects.

G.D.M.

THE TITS

The Tit family are small, dumpy, acrobatic birds with short beaks and strong feet. The male and female birds are similar in colour. They mostly nest in holes and tree cavities, and will happily use nesting boxes and bird tables.

1 The Crested Tit

A small bird, $4\frac{1}{2}$ ins. long, in Gt. Britain it is found only in the Spey valley in Scotland, so you may never see one for yourself. It has a pointed speckled crest, brown upper parts with darker wings, and dull white under-parts, white cheeks and black facial markings.

2 The Coal Tit

A common tit found throughout Britain, in wooded country and in gardens. It is $4\frac{1}{2}$ ins. long, short-tailed, and its distinguishing feature is a large white spot on the nape of its neck. It has a glossy black head, throat and neck and white cheeks. Its under-parts are buff coloured and its back and wings are dark brown. It has a black bill and dark legs.

3 The Blue Tit

This very popular tit, also called 'Tom-Tit', is a friendly aggressive bird, about $4\frac{1}{2}$ ins. long. It lives near houses, in lanes or in thick woods. It is a destroyer of pests, but also damages young buds in its search for insects. Its blue crown is well-known. It has a dark line through its eye and round its white cheeks to its chin. The neck, wings and tail are all blue, its back is yellow-green, and its underparts a bright yellow with a dark line down its middle.

4 The Great Tit

This larger, sparrow-sized tit, $5\frac{1}{2}$ ins. long, is seen all over Britain. Its head and neck are a glossy blue-black, its cheeks white, and upper parts greenish blue-grey. It can be recognised by a black stripe down its yellow underparts, from its chin almost to its tail. It has a rasping, squeaky song, sounding like 'pee-ker' – pee-ker', and its diet is a variety of insects, seeds, and nuts.

1 The Marsh Tit

One of the two black-headed tits to be found in Britain, the Marsh Tit is 4½ ins. long. Both sexes are alike and have glossy black heads, short black bibs, white cheeks, and greyish white underparts. The back is a sandy brown colour, the wings and square tail are grey-brown, the beak is black, and the legs are lead coloured. This tit is found in damp marshy places, but is also common in dry woods, hedgerows and gardens. Its food is animal or vegetable – weevils, beetles, larvae, as well as seeds of all kinds. Its characteristic song is a harsh, repeated 'cheevi-cheevi'.

2 The Willow Tit

This is the other common black-headed tit found in Britain. 4½ ins. long, it is distinguished from the Marsh Tit by its sooty, instead of glossy black head; and a tail that is more graduated than the square tail of the Marsh Tit. Otherwise both tits look alike, and are found in the same sort of country. The Willow Tits song is a long drawn out 'zee, zee, zee'.

3 The Long-tailed Tit

This tiny, but long-tailed bird is found in woods, thickets, parks and gardens all over Britain. It builds its beautifully constructed, domed, lichen-covered nests in bushes or forks of trees. The head of the Long-tailed Tit is dull white, banded with black above the eye. The nape of its neck and upper back are black and its shoulders and rump are a pink colour. Its wings are brownish black with white edges, and its outer tail feathers have white margins and tips. Its underparts are white. It is 5½ ins. long including its tail.

4 The Bearded Tit

This is not a common tit in Britain. It is now found only on the Norfolk Broads, and in parts of Devon, in reed beds by streams and lakes. 5½ ins. long, its upper parts are a tawny brown colour and it has a long graduated tail. The male bird has a black 'moustache' and black feathers on the underside of its tail. Its head is blue-grey with greyish white chin, throat, and breast, and it has an orange bill.

WARBLERS AND THEIR ALLIES

Warblers are small, active, rather dull-coloured song-birds, with slender pointed bills. Their songs are varied and distinctive. They are solitary birds, and are usually found in places where there is dense vegetation. Their diet consists of insects. In most species the sexes look alike.

The Willow Warbler

The Willow Warbler, or Willow Wren, is one of our most common residents. It is one of the three 'leaf warblers' found in woods, parks and gardens in Britain. The other two are the Wood Warbler and the Chiff-Chaff. The Willow Warbler is $4\frac{1}{4}$ ins. long, with olive green upperparts, pale yellow underparts, white belly and brown bill and legs. Its song is a musical, liquid warble, starting softly and ending in a descending scale.

The Chiff-chaff (*not illustrated*)

This 'leaf warbler' is very like the Willow Warbler in looks and habits. Its plumage is a duller colour, the upperparts being olive brown and underparts a dirty white, and its legs are a blacker brown. Unlike the Willow Wren, its song is a monotonous 'chiff-chaff'.

The Wood Warbler (*not illustrated*)

Larger (5 ins.) and more slender than the Willow Warbler and the Chiff-Chaff. It is common in deciduous and mixed woods.

The Wood Warbler (*continued*)

It has yellow-green upperparts and a clear yellow throat and breast, white belly, and a yellow stripe above the eye. Its song is a long trilling 'stip, stip, stip' sound.

1 The Marsh Warbler

An inconspicuous bird, found in reeds and marshes. 5 ins. long, with olive brown upperparts, yellow-white underparts and pale pink legs. It has a musical song and is a mimic.

2 The Sedge Warbler

Very common in thickets and swamps and wet places all over Britain. Its streaked back and distinct cream coloured eyestripe distinguish it from other warblers. It is 5 ins. long.

3 The Grasshopper Warbler

Common in England, in water meadows and bushy land. It is 5 ins. long with a broad wedged-shaped tail, streaked olive-brown back and wings, and whitish grey underside. It seldom flies in the open.

4 The Reed Warbler
(*not illustrated*)

Very similar to the Marsh Warbler but browner on the upperparts. Underparts are whitish-buff, bill and legs are dark brown. Its song is harsh and it sings both day and night.

1 The Blackcap

A common Summer visitor, seen in woods with dense undergrowth. 5½ ins. long, the male's cap is black, the female's chestnut, upperparts grey-brown, under-parts pale grey, and song a rich warble.

2 The Garden Warbler

Found in gardens, parks and woods, this 5½ ins. long bird has olive-brown upperparts, grey-white underparts, and a mellow warbling song.

3 The Dartford Warbler

Now only seen in southern England, this bird is 5 ins. long, dark brown above and reddish below, with spotted chin and throat, and a cocked tail.

4 The Goldcrest

Our smallest bird, 3¼ ins. long. Fairly rare, it likes coniferous woods and copses. It has a black-bordered, yellow-topped head, lime green upperparts, dull white underparts and two white wing bars.

5 The Whitethroat

A Summer visitor, this slender, active brown-grey bird 5½ ins. long, has a white throat and chin and white outer tail feathers. **The Lesser Whitethroat** is similar but smaller with a shorter tail.

THE FLYCATCHERS

These small birds have short beaks. They perch upright, waiting to catch passing insects on the wing.

1 The Pied Flycatcher

A Summer visitor found in woods and parks in Western and Northern counties of England. 5 ins. long, the male has black upperparts and white underparts, with white patches on his wings. The female is brown and white.

2 The Spotted Flycatcher

A Summer visitor to woods, parks and gardens. 5½ ins. long, brownish grey with dark speckles on forehead and breast, dull white underparts. Its tail flicks continuously.

THRUSHES AND THEIR ALLIES

These are long-legged, medium-sized birds, with slender pointed beaks, long wings and tails. They feed mainly on the ground, eating worms, insects and fruit. Their song is melodious. They build open cup-shaped nests in trees or bushes.

Fieldfares and Redwings (*not illustrated*)

Winter visitors to Britain, arriving late September, and leaving March to early May. The Fieldfare is larger (10 ins.) than the Redwing (8 ins.). Both birds have speckled breasts – the Fieldfare has a grey head and rump, and the Redwing has a creamy eye stripe, and chestnut underwings.

1 The Song Thrush

One of our best known birds, seen everywhere in gardens, hedges and woods. 8½ ins. long, with olive brown underparts, light buff, dark speckled underparts, dark bill and brown legs. Has a sweet song; eggs very blue with black spots.

2 The Mistle Thrush

The largest of the thrushes, – 11 ins. long – like the Song Thrush, but the speckles on its underparts are dark brown ovals, and its song is less melodious. Its eggs are greenish-white, blotched with purple-brown.

3 The Blackbird

This familiar garden bird is 10 ins. long. The male is glossy black with yellow bill; the female dark brown, with dark speckles on light buff throat and breast. Its song is flute-like. Eggs, greenish-white, speckled red-brown.

4 The Nightingale

This night-singing bird, beloved of poets, is 6½ ins. long, with russet brown upperparts, dull white underparts, and brown bill and legs. It lives in leafy woods, thickets, and hedges, in Southern England only. Its olive brown eggs are laid at ground level in nests of leaves and grass.

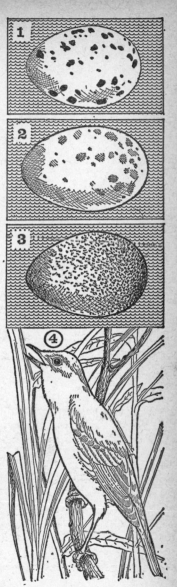

1 The Wheatear

This bird is a Summer visitor, $5\frac{1}{2}$ ins. long, frequenting downs, hillsides and open country. It is recognisable by its distinctive black and white tail – black tipped with long black central feathers. The male has a grey back and crown, black wings and a black 'eye patch', and creamy buff underparts. The female is sandy brown above, buff below and has the same black and white tail.

2 The Whinchat

Smaller than a sparrow ($5\frac{1}{2}$ ins. long), this bird is a Summer visitor, and found on commons, open heaths, and grasslands. A stocky bird with dark-streaked grey-brown upperparts and russet throat and breast. It has a white stripe above the eye and below the black cheek, a white patch on its brown wings, and white side feathers to its tail.

3 The Stonechat

Seen on commons and gorseland, mainly in coastal areas of Britain, this bird is 5 ins. long, with blackish brown upperparts, black head and throat, white sides to its neck, white wing stripe, dark tail and a rust-red breast. The female is a duller colour.

1 **The Redstart** *and the* **Black Redstart** (*not illustrated*)
The Redstart is a woodland bird, particularly liking old timber.
5½ ins. long, the male has a slate-grey head and upperparts,
breast, sides and tail rust-red and white forehead and line
above the eye. The face and throat are black. The female is
browner. The black Redstart is a winter visitor, similar to the
Redstart, but darker, and with different Winter haunts – it
likes cliffs and rocky places.

2 The Robin
This well-loved bird has absolute trust in man. It is found all
over Britain, in gardens and farmyards. It is 5¾ ins. long, with a
rounded body and long legs. There is a narrow blue-grey
margin between the olive-brown upperparts, and the red
breast and throat. It has beady black eyes and brown legs.

1 The Dipper

This large, round, short-tailed bird, 7 ins. long, lives near swiftly running water. It has long legs, short wings, and is slate-grey colour, with a white throat and chest, a red-brown belly and a black beak.

2 The Wren

One of our smallest birds, $3\frac{1}{2}$ ins. long, with a round body, short tail and wings. Its brown plumage is barred with darker brown. Its mouse-like look makes it hard to see. Lives in woods and gardens.

3 The Hedge Sparrow

Also called a Dunnock, this bird, $5\frac{3}{4}$ ins. long, with brown, black-streaked plumage, and slate-grey head, lives in hedges and gardens.

4 The Kingfisher

This waterside bird, feeding on aquatic animals, is about $7\frac{1}{2}$ ins. long, with metallic blue upperparts, green head and wings. Its underparts and ear coverts are rust-red, chin and sides of neck are white. Long black bill with orange base. Plunges under water for fish.

THE WOODPECKERS

This family of birds have 'yoked' feet – two toes point backwards, two forwards. They have strong pointed bills and long tongues for picking insects out of holes in tree-trunks. You can often hear them 'drumming' with their beaks.

1 The Green Woodpecker

The largest of our woodpeckers, 12 ins. long, with green upperparts and a chrome-yellow rump. The crown of its head is crimson, cheeks and round the eyes are black. It has bars of black and white on its side wings. Common in deciduous woods in England and Wales.

2 The Great Spotted Woodpecker

A Winter visitor to deciduous and coniferous woods. A handsome, 9 ins. long, black and white bird with a red spot on the nape of its neck, a red belly and red under tail feathers.

3 The Lesser Spotted Woodpecker

The smallest woodpecker, 6 ins. long, rare in North and West England but seen elsewhere. It has a crimson crown, black and white barred back, wings and tail, and white underparts.

1 THE SWIFTS

Swifts look like swallows, but are not related. They are 6½ ins. long, high flying, blackish-brown birds, with white chins.

THE SWALLOWS

These graceful, endlessly flying birds have long pointed wings, and forked tails.

2 The Swallow

A Summer visitor to farms and open country, it is a blue-black bird, 7 ins. long with deeply forked tail, red throat and white underparts.

3 The House Martin

A small bird, 5 ins. long, with a short, slightly forked tail, white throat, underparts and rump. Seen in villages and farms.

4 The Sand Martin

Our smallest swallow, 5 ins. long, with a slightly forked tail, earth-brown upperparts, white underparts and grey-brown collar. Found near river banks, cliffs, and gravel pits.

THE PIGEONS AND DOVES

These medium-sized, heavy birds have short bills, pointed wings, and they are sociable.

1 The Wood Pigeon

Our largest pigeon, 16 ins. long, a familiar grey-blue bird with a white patch on the side of its purple-green neck, and a white band across its wings.

2 The Stock Dove

Smaller than a Wood Pigeon, 13 ins. long, with no white feathers; likes open country.

3 The Rock Dove

Not a common pigeon, this 13 ins. long bird has a white rump and two black wing bands.

4 The Turtle Dove

A small, shy, slim pigeon, 11 ins. long, common in farmland and woods. Upperparts red-brown, black and white stripes on its neck, and grey-white underparts.

The Collared Dove (*not shown*) first seen here in 1955.

G.D.M.

1 THE CUCKOO

'The Cuckoo sings in April' is the beginning of a favourite nursery jingle, and 'the first cuckoo' to be heard each year is eagerly recorded. A Summer visitor to woods and gardens, it is a large, shy bird, 13 ins. long, with slate-grey upperparts, lighter underparts darkly barred, very pointed wings, and yellow legs. It is 'parasitic', laying one egg at a time in the nests of other song birds, who then hatch and feed the baby cuckoos. Its song 'cuckoo' is easily recognisable.

2 THE NIGHTJAR

Mostly seen at dusk, when its churring trill is heard; this bird is a late Summer visitor. 11 ins. long with big eyes, plumage the colour of bark and dead leaves.

THE OWLS

Owls are nocturnal birds of prey. They have big heads, flat faces, and their eyes are forward facing. They fly silently, hunting for rodents, small mammals, birds and insects. Call is a hoot, whistle or wail.

1 The Long-eared Owl

Common in fir woods, this 13 ins. owl has very long ear tufts. Buff upperparts with grey-brown speckles, underparts rusty yellow, darkly streaked.

2 The Short-eared Owl

Seen in open country, moors and marshes, a 15 ins. owl with nearly invisible ears, and buff plumage, streaked and blotched with darker brown.

3 The Tawny Owl

This woodland bird, 15 ins. long, sleeps during the day. It has a greyish round face, large dark eyes, no ear-tufts, and mottled brown plumage.

4 The Little Owl

A small, squat, fierce-looking, flat headed bird, 9 ins. long. Grey-brown upper-parts whitish-brown streaks below.

5 The Barn Owl

Sandy coloured, 14 ins. long, with a white heart-shaped face, and long legs, this owl likes farms, old buildings and ruins.

75

BIRDS OF PREY

Birds of Prey are flesh-eaters, with heavy, sharp, hooked beaks, and long, strong, curved talons on powerful toes, used to seize and hold their prey. The wing positions in flight, as shown above, help to identify the different species.

1 The Golden Eagle

This noble, golden brown bird is now only found in the Scottish Highlands and the Hebrides. Its wing span can be 90 ins. Powerful body, curved, hooked beak, large feet, feathered legs.

2 The Buzzard

Found on rocky coasts, moors and mountains, this bird has a 54 in. wing span. Its beak is sharp and hooked. Its colour varies but is usually dark brown, with a whitish brown barred breast.

3 The Sparrow-Hawk

Resident in woods all over Britain, smaller than the buzzard – 31 in. wing span. It has slate-grey upperparts, dark brown, grey-barred tail feathers, and rusty barred underparts. The female's breast is white barred brown.

76

1 The Montague Harrier

A rare visitor to marshes and moors in S.W. England and Scotland, this bird has a 40 ins. wing span. The male is blue-grey above with black wing tips and wing bar, white underparts with brown streaks. The female is brown.

2 The Hen Harrier

Another bird of passage. Large, with a wing span of 40–43 ins. The male's upperparts, throat and breast are grey, with no black wing stripes. Underparts are white. The female is brown.

3 The Peregrine Falcon

Our largest, most powerful falcon, found near rocky coasts. Black moustachial stripe. Upperparts slate-grey, whitish underparts with dark markings. Wing span 32–44 ins.

4 The Kestrel

The most common and widespread British falcon, found in open woods, moors and even in cities. It has a slate-grey head and nape, chestnut back, slate tail with black band and black spotted buff underparts. Wing span 24–26 ins.

5 The Merlin

Found on moors in N. Britain, it has a 24–26ins. wing span, slate-blue upperparts, and brown-streaked, buff, underparts.

WATER FOWL

In this section we have put all the birds that you might see near lakes, ponds and rivers in this country. The Swans, Geese and Ducks; the Herons and Bitterns; the Coots, and the Grebes.

SWANS

These are large white, long-necked swimming birds. They dip their head and neck under water to feed on the bottom vegetation. They have short legs and a waddling gait.

The female is called a pen, the male is a cob, and the young swans are called cygnets and when very small often ride on their parents' backs.

1 The Whooper Swan

A Winter visitor to N. and W. of Scotland, when swimming this swan carries its neck stiffly erect and does not raise its wing feathers. It is 58 ins. long. Its yellow, black-tipped beak has no knob. The Bewick Swan (not illustrated) is similar to the Whooper, but not so large.

2 The Mute Swan

The most widespread of our swans, 58 ins. long with a 95 in. wing span. Has a graceful S curved neck and a black knob at the base of its orange bill. Its flight is slow and powerful. The young swans are grey until they are nearly three years old.

HERONS AND BITTERNS

These birds are all wading birds with long legs, straight bills, and slow flight.

1 The Grey or Common Heron

You can see this elegant large bird standing upright by any area of open water, fresh or salt, in Britain. It is 36 ins. long, with a wing-span of 55 ins. Its plumage is ash-grey, with darker grey flight feathers, white forehead, head and neck, with black markings, and trailing black crest. In flight its neck is drawn in in an 'S' shape, and its legs trail behind.

2 The Bittern

This brown, mottled bird is an inhabitant of reed beds. Its normal position is a crouching one, but when alarmed it will freeze into a tall 'stick' with its body rigid, head back, and neck outstretched. It is a rare bird and very elusive. It is 30 ins. long, with a short tail. Its broad wings span 50 ins. and its tail is short. It rests by day and becomes active at dusk and during the night.

79

The Teal, 14 ins. long, 21 in. wing span, this small attractive bird has a white, black-edged stripe on his wing, a chestnut head, and metallic green eye stripe, edged white. Seen in most counties.

The Pintail, 14 ins. long with wing span 35 ins., a slim bird, with long neck, and pointed tail. Head and back of its neck are chocolate, breast and front neck white, and upperparts grey.

The Shoveller, 20 ins. long, wing-span 31 ins., is seen everywhere. It has a broad 'shovel' beak. The drake's head is glossy green, neck and breast white, chestnut underparts, and blue wing patch.

The Shelduck (*not shown*) is a large, black, white and chestnut goose-like bird. Seen on sandy coasts all over Britain.

BAY DUCKS

These surface-diving ducks have plump bodies and short thick necks. They swim under water and run along the surface when taking off. They nest on lake shores and in swamps.

The Pochard, 18 ins. long, 31 in. wing-span, is a sociable red-headed duck, with a light grey body, and black breast. It is seen on eastern coasts of Britain.

The Tufted Duck, 17 ins. long, with a 28 in. wing span, has black and white plumage and a long black heron-like crest. It is common in all parts of Britain.

Bay Ducks (*cont'd*)

The Scaup 18 ins. long, 31 ins. wing-span. Mainly a Winter visitor, with a black head and breast, grey back and white belly.

SEA DUCKS

Large ducks living on our coast and diving for food on sea bed.

The Common Eider, 20 ins. long, wings 41 ins., has a white back, black belly, pink breast and white black-crowned head and sloping profile. Seen on Scottish coasts.

The Common Scoter, 20 ins. long, wings 33 ins., a quite black duck, it nests in Scotland and a common visitor elsewhere.

MERGANSERS

These are fish-eating ducks, with crested heads, long bills and slender bodies. Live on lakes, rivers and reservoirs.

The Goosander, 25 ins. long, wings 37 ins. The largest of this group, its head and neck are greenish-black, breast and belly white. Seen in N. England and Scotland.

The Red-Breasted Merganser, 22 ins. long, wings 33 ins., with red beak, black head, metallic green neck, white collar, black back, russet breast.

WATER RAILS, CRAKES AND COOTS

These birds are medium-sized to small, neatly built, with short necks, long legs and long toes. Some of them (the Moorhen and Coot) have swimming membranes on their toes. The Rails and Crakes are secretive, the Coots are sociable.

1 The Spotted Crake

A rare Summer visitor, 9 ins. long, this dull olive-brown bird has a short tail and beak. Skulks in ponds and marshes.

2 The Water Rail

A dull grey-brown bird, 11 ins. long with slender beak and long legs. Secretive, so seldom seen, it breeds in most British marshes.

3 The Corncrake

A Summer visitor to fields and meadows, this 10 in. long slender brown bird has chestnut wings, barred flanks and a short bill.

4 The Moorhen

Common on lakes and ponds everywhere this 13 in. long black bird has a red frontal beak shield, white line on its flanks, and white under tail feathers used as a danger signal.

5 The Coot

Also a common black water bird, 15 ins. long, it has a white frontal beak shield and bill, and no white tail feathers.

GREBES

These are slender, fish-eating diving birds, with lobed and partially webbed toes. Their short legs are placed far back on the body. They have elaborate courtship displays, during which they become very vocal. They live on lakes and rivers.

1 The Little Grebe, also called a Dabchick, 10 ins. long, russet head and neck, other parts black, no crest. Common, but very shy.

2 The Black-necked Grebe, 12 ins. long, has a golden tuft on its cheek, glossy black neck and body, and rich chestnut flanks.

3 The Slavonian Grebe, is a rare Winter visitor, 23 ins. long, with 'horns' of gold feathers, white belly, dark body and chestnut flanks.

4 The Great crested Grebe, is a large bird 18 ins. long with long straight neck, with chestnut and black 'frills', upperparts grey-brown, belly, white. On lakes and meres everywhere.

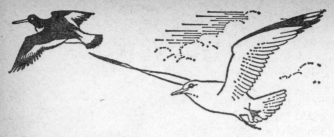

SHORE BIRDS, GULLS AND AUKS

A great many different birds belong to this group all of which are water birds; either swimming (the gulls, the auks and the phalaropes) or wading (the oystercatchers, and all the other shore birds).

THE SHORE BIRDS

These birds vary from small to medium-sized. They have short bills, long legs, and long pointed wings. The sexes are similar and they are often seen in large flocks. Their courtship behaviour is often very elaborate, and their nests are usually made on the ground.

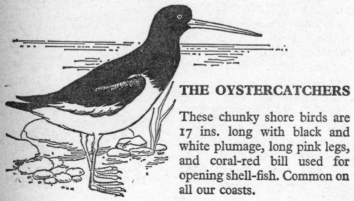

THE OYSTERCATCHERS

These chunky shore birds are 17 ins. long with black and white plumage, long pink legs, and coral-red bill used for opening shell-fish. Common on all our coasts.

1 The Lapwing or 'Pee-wit'

This glossy greenish-black and white crested bird, 12 ins. long is seen in meadows, marshes, and moors, often in flocks, all over Britain. Unlike other waders, it has broad rounded wings.

2 The Ringed Plover

Of the 2 similar Ringed plovers, the larger (7 ins.) is more common on our shores. Its upperparts are mouse-grey, underparts and throat white, cheek and eyeband, and breast patch are black.

3 The Kentish Plover

A rare visitor, 6 ins. long, sandy grey on upper parts, white forehead, streak above eye and underparts. It has black patch on its forehead and neck.

4 The Dotterel

A rare Summer visitor, seen in the Scottish Highlands and the Lake District. Its back and wings are brownish-grey. A white band divides the brown breast and orange-brown underparts. It has a white throat and face.

5 The Golden Plover

Seen in many parts of Britain, 11 ins. long, it has dark upper parts mottled in gold. The underparts, from cheek to tail are black, divided from wings by a white stripe.

SNIPE AND WOODCOCK

Although belonging to the same family as the Plovers, these are inland birds of woods, marshes and river banks. They are secretive, have long straight bills, short necks and legs.

1 The Snipe

This night-feeding bird, 10 ins. long, lives in our marshes and water meadows. It has brown-black upperparts, streaked with yellow, white underparts, throat and breast grey, brown-flecked. Its bill is soft-tipped.

2 The Woodcock

A shy nocturnal bird of the woods, 14 ins. long, the colour of dead leaves, with big, set-back eyes and a long beak.

CURLEWS AND GODWITS

Two groups of long legged shore birds, (1) Curlews, brown with down-turned bills; (2) Godwits, reddish, with up-turned bills.

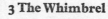

3 The Whimbrel

A rare Summer visitor to Britain, smaller than the Curlew (16 ins.), and with a shorter bill.

4 The Curlew

A fairly common 22 in. bird with long curved bill. Nests on marshes, moors and mud-flats. Call – a mellow whistle 'curlee'.

5 The Black-tailed Godwit

This uncommon, reddish bird lives on mud-flats and shores. Has an upturned bill.

1 The Stone Curlew

Britain's only bird in this group. A rather ungainly Summer visitor, 16 ins. long, with round head and large yellow eyes. Sandy-brown, dark-streaked back, paler underparts, and white wing bars. Nocturnal in habit, it lives in bare, stony barren places.

2 The Common Sandpiper

A very common bird, seen on freshwater as well as salt-water shores. Its back is olive brown, darkly streaked, it has white underparts, and white and brown barred tail feathers. Its tail bobs continuously as it explores the water's edge.

3 The Greenshank

Summer visitors, but some nest in N. Scotland. 12 ins. long, with dark grey upper parts, and lighter below, a white rump, green legs and slightly upturned bill.

4 The Redshank

Seen on marshes, both coast and inland everywhere, this white-rumped bird is 11 ins. long. Its body is brown, with white wing bars and it has red legs.

5 The Spotted Redshank

A large rare blackish bird, white flecked, 12 ins. long, with red legs.

SMALL SANDPIPERS
1 The Dunlin A brown shore bird, 7 ins. long, with a large black patch on its belly. It nests on moors and marshes.

PHALAROPES
2 The Red-necked Phalarope A rare visitor to Scotland, $6\frac{1}{2}$ ins. long, brown, with white chin and belly, chestnut neck.

DIVERS Large water birds with webbed feet.

3 The Red-throated Diver

A rare Winter visitor to coasts in Britain, but breeds only in N. Scotland. The smallest Diver, 22 ins. long, with grey head and upper parts, white belly, black and white stripes on its neck, and a red throat.

4 The Black-throated Diver

Also a rare Winter visitor, breeding in N. Scotland. 25 ins. long with grey head, black throat, thin black stripes on the sides of its neck, and on its breast. The black upperparts have white striped patches, and the belly is white.

GULLS

These are sturdy birds, living by the sea, battling with storms and winds. They have long pointed wings, webbed feet, and strong hooked bills. The sexes look alike. They are scavengers.

1 The Common Gull

Seen on all our coasts, but breeding only in Scotland and Ireland, this gull is 16 ins. long, head, neck, tail, and underparts are white, wings blue-grey, black and white tipped; beak is yellow.

2 The Great Black-backed Gull

Common along all our coasts, but rarely seen inland, this big bird, 27 ins. long, has a dark grey back and wings. The tips of its wing feathers, head, tail, underparts and neck are white. The heavy beak is yellow with a red tip to the lower part. Legs are flesh pink.

3 The Lesser Black-backed Gull

A similar but smaller bird than (2), this gull has yellow legs. Its back and wings are a light grey.

G.D.M.

1 The Herring Gull
You see these gulls everywhere on our coasts, and even inland, following the plough. Smaller than the Black-headed Gulls, 22 ins. long, with back and wings pearl-grey, head, neck, tail and underparts white, and outer wing feathers black with white tips. You often see them paddling in wet sand at the water's edge, or dropping crabs etc., onto rocks to smash them.

2 The Black-headed Gull
Slim and sociable, only 14 ins. long, its tapering wings have a white leading edge, and black tips. Short neck, crimson beak and legs, and blue-grey back and wings. Its chocolate head gives it its name. Also follows the plough.

3 The Kittiwake
A gull of the cliffs and open sea, 14 ins. long, with blue-grey back and wings, otherwise snowy white, except for black-tipped outer wing feathers, greeny-yellow bill and black legs.

SKUAS

These fierce sea-birds look like large, dark gulls with elongated central tail feathers. Piratical, they rob other birds of fish. They are offshore birds, only nesting on land.

1 The Great Skua

Only seen in Scotland and the Scottish Islands, this large brown bird, 23 ins. long, with a 5 ft. wing span, has white wing patches, formed by the base of its 'primary' feathers and only slightly projecting central tail feathers.

2 The Arctic Skua

The most common skua, more elegant than the Great Skua, and smaller (18 ins. long, 3 ft. 6 ins. wing span). There are 2 different forms: the dark type, ashy-brown all over with slightly paler underparts; and the light type, with white or cream neck and underparts. They are seen, often in large numbers, off the coasts of Scotland and the Scottish Islands.

TERNS

Slender birds with sharp beaks, long narrow wings, forked tails, short legs and webbed feet. Mostly black and white in colour, their plumage differs from Summer to Winter. They dive from the air for their food.

1 The Common Tern

A 14 in. long, white bird, with pearl-grey back and wings. The Summer cap is black, beak orange, black tipped; in the Winter it has a white forehead, and the beak is almost black.

2 The Arctic Tern

Similar to the Common Tern, but with no black tip to red beak. Common in Scotland and Ireland, rare elsewhere.

3 The Sandwich Tern

Our largest Tern, 16 ins. long, in Summer has black-crested head, black beak, yellow tipped; in Winter head is streaked.

4 The Little Tern

Our rare smallest tern (9 ins. long) has a white forehead, black crown, yellow legs and beak, the latter black tipped.

AUKS

This family of stout, black and white, salt-water, diving birds have short tails, short narrow wings, and webbed feet. On land they have an erect posture. They swim under water, and only come ashore to breed, when they nest on cliffs and rocks. Their diet is small fish. Sadly, the Great Auk is now extinct.

1 The Razorbill
The thick beak of this 16 in. long bird has pressed-in sides, and a white stripe from eye to tip. Its plumage is black above with white wing bars, breast and belly. Nests in colonies on suitable sea-cliffs.

2 The Guillemot
At nesting time this bird gathers in large numbers on our coastal cliffs. 16 ins. long it has a slim pointed beak, deep brown upperparts, thin white wing bars, and a white 'shirt front'.

3 The Black Guillemot
Smaller and rarer than (2), this 13 in. long, brownish black bird has a white wing patch, and red feet. Seen singly, or in small numbers, breeding mainly in Scotland.

4 The Puffin
This 12 in. long bird is seen, in large numbers, on cliffs all round Britain. Its triangular red, blue and yellow beak and deep-set eye, in a white face, give it a comic look. Black and white plumage, orange feet.

BIRDS OF THE OCEAN

Tubenoses

These birds come ashore only to breed, when they nest in colonies on remote islands and lonely coastlines. They are called 'Tubenoses' because, in place of slits in the upper beak, they have tube-shaped external nostrils. With long narrow wings they fly near the surface of the sea, feeding on small fish, plankton and scraps from ships. The sexes have similar plumage.

1 The Fulmar

This large gull-like bird, 18 ins. long, with a 42 in. wing span, nests on high cliff-top ledges on all our North Atlantic coasts. A white bird, with silver grey back and wings, heavy head, short neck, and a graceful gliding flight, it follows ships often for long distances, scarcely ever coming in to land.

96

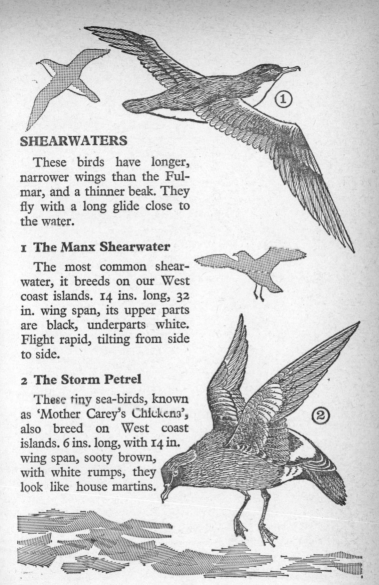

SHEARWATERS

These birds have longer, narrower wings than the Fulmar, and a thinner beak. They fly with a long glide close to the water.

1 The Manx Shearwater

The most common shearwater, it breeds on our West coast islands. 14 ins. long, 32 in. wing span, its upper parts are black, underparts white. Flight rapid, tilting from side to side.

2 The Storm Petrel

These tiny sea-birds, known as 'Mother Carey's Chickens', also breed on West coast islands. 6 ins. long, with 14 in. wing span, sooty brown, with white rumps, they look like house martins.

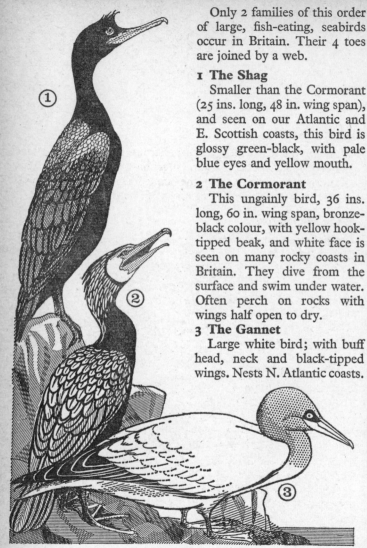

Only 2 families of this order of large, fish-eating, seabirds occur in Britain. Their 4 toes are joined by a web.

1 The Shag

Smaller than the Cormorant (25 ins. long, 48 in. wing span), and seen on our Atlantic and E. Scottish coasts, this bird is glossy green-black, with pale blue eyes and yellow mouth.

2 The Cormorant

This ungainly bird, 36 ins. long, 60 in. wing span, bronze-black colour, with yellow hook-tipped beak, and white face is seen on many rocky coasts in Britain. They dive from the surface and swim under water. Often perch on rocks with wings half open to dry.

3 The Gannet

Large white bird; with buff head, neck and black-tipped wings. Nests N. Atlantic coasts.

GAME BIRDS

All these birds are heavy-bodied ground birds, with short rounded wings, short beaks, and most have feathered legs. The cocks are more splendid than the hens. They feed on seeds and insects, which they forage for on the ground.

1 The Red Grouse

Truly British, only found on these islands. It is a moorland bird, 13 ins.–15 ins. long, with dark red-brown plumage, white feathered legs, and a red patch, called a wattle, above its eye. It nests on the ground among heather and bracken.

2 The Ptarmigan

A bird of high mountains, only found above the tree-line in Scotland and the Western Isles. 14 ins. long, it changes its plumage with the seasons, from barred brown and grey upperparts, white underparts, in Spring – to grey, black barred upperparts in Autumn – and white all over with black outer tail feathers in Winter.

1 The Capercaillie

This large bird, extinct here since 1750, was re-introduced to Scottish conifer woods, in 1837. The male, 24 ins. long, has a fan-shaped tail, black body, brown back and yellow beak. Red wattle above eyes.

2 The Black Grouse

Seen at dawn or dusk, among moorland trees in N. Devon, Somerset, Wales and N. England. The male, 21 ins. long, and glossy black, with lyre-shape tail; the female 18 ins., and brown-grey. Both have red eye 'wattles'.

3 The Red-legged Partridge

It is $13\frac{1}{2}$ ins. long, with white face outlined in black-brown, black and white barred wings, red legs and beak.

4 The Partridge

Our most common game-bird, seen on farmland every-where, 12 ins. long, with a short, rusty tail, orange-brown head and throat, and chestnut patch on its belly.

5 The Quail

Our smallest game-bird, 7 ins. long. A shy ground dwel-ler, only moving at sunset. Its plumage is buff, with black-streaked back, yellow-streaked wings and flank. The male has a brown throat stripe.

The Pheasant

Two varieties of this bird live in Britain – one with a white neck-ring, introduced from China in the 1700's; one with no ring, introduced before 1050. The cock, 33 ins. long, is more colourful, with head and neck green shot with blue, and body reddish brown, shot purple. The female, 23 ins. long, is mottled brown. Both have long pointed tails.

* * *

There are some birds which, if you are very lucky, you may see in our countryside. These are named by the British Ornithologists Union, in their 1971 list of British Birds, as scarce or Winter visitors. They are only seen rarely, and in special areas, or at particular times of the year. Here is a list:—

Winter Visitors		Summer and Scarce Visitors	
Great Northern Diver	Iceland Gull	Spoonbill	Little Bunting
Red necked Grebe	Little Gull	Avocet	Serin
Bewicks Swan	Little Auk	Osprey	Tawny Pippit
Brent Goose	Waxwing	Hobby	Little Stint
Barnacle Goose	Firecrest	Wryneck	Hoopoe
Golden eye Duck	Brambling	Tree-Pippit	Red Kite
Velvet Scoter	Shore-lark	Ring Ouzel	Honey
Grey Plover	Water Pippit	Nutcracker	Buzzard
Knott	Ruff	Golden Oriole	

BUTTERFLIES TO LOOK FOR

There are 68 different kinds of butterfly in Britain, but we can only show you 45. We have chosen the most common ones, and drawn them life-size, describing their colours and stating their habitat. Unfortunately unsettled weather, over populated countrysides, and mechanical farming all mean that Britain is not an ideal country for these beautiful creatures, who depend on sunshine and special environments for survival, and their numbers decrease every year. Many are only found in a few places, and some, for instance the Large Copper, only seen in Wood Walton Fen in Huntingdonshire, are now almost extinct.

Butterflies and moths belong to the order Lepidopteria – the butterflies can be identified by their 'clubbed' feelers.

Three distinct changes are gone through before the butterfly achieves its final form:– (1) the egg, (2) the caterpillar and (3) the chrysalis. We cannot show you all these stages, different in each species, but one example, the Large White, is opposite. In the caterpillar stage the insect is very selective, often only feeding on one kind of plant, so the female lays her eggs on this plant; for example you will see the Small Tortoiseshell on Stinging Nettles, and the Brown Hairstreak on Blackthorn.

Butterflies can distinguish colours, and prefer purple or blue flowers. Their own bright colour helps them to recognise each other, but the undersides of their wings are more subdued and, when folded protect them, by camouflage, from their enemies.

The Life Cycle of the Large White Butterfly

1 The Large White, or Cabbage White lays its eggs on various cruciferous plants, such as Wild or Garden Cabbage, Hedge Mustard, Radish or Turnip. Laid in batches, varying in size from 6 to 100, the eggs are yellow, and shaped like a ribbed skittle. They take about 7 days, in summer, to hatch.

(enlarged)

2 The caterpillars, when fully grown, are greenish, and about 1¾ ins. long. When small they live in groups feeding on the surface of the cabbage leaves. Like all caterpillars their skins cannot stretch, so, to allow for growth, they shed their skins at intervals and grow new ones. After the first shedding, they begin to eat holes in the food leaves, and when two-thirds grown the group disperses and the caterpillars feed singly.

3 Now it is time for the caterpillar to prepare for the next stage – the chrysalis. It stops eating, shrinks in size and spins a silk pad beneath its hind legs and a girdle round its waist to keep it in position against a fence or a wall. In a few days its skin splits and the chrysalis emerges. The chrysalis is grey coloured with black spots, and is unable to move. The outline of wings, legs, tongue etc., can be seen on the outside of the shell.

4 In about 3 weeks (the time varies for species and for seasons) the butterfly is ready to emerge. The shell splits behind the head and the insect frees itself.

THE BROWNS

1 The Grayling*
This butterfly, seen all over Britain, haunts rough fields and exposed places. Brown, with black shading, it has light bands on its wings. The fore wings have 2 white-centred spots and there is 1 black spot at the base of the hind wings. The underside of these wings is earth-coloured, and on alighting the insect falls sideways, towards the soil, camouflaged.

2 The Hedge Brown*
Another orange-brown butterfly, with dark margins to its wings. The fore wings have a black spot at the tip, often with 2 white dots, and there's usually a white-centred spot on the hind wings. Seen in August and September, in hedgerows and among brambles, in Southern England.

3 The Meadow Brown*
One of our most common butterflies, seen in fields and in meadows everywhere, from June to September. It is dark blackish-brown with a large black, white-centred, orange-circled eye-spot on each fore wing.

4 The Small Heath*
This small butterfly is found, from late May to early October, in grassy places, even up to 2,000 feet above sea-level, everywhere in Britain. The wings are tawny-yellow, with brown borders, and a black spot at the tip of each fore wing.

5 The Large Heath*
A butterfly found only on bogs and mosses in Northern Britain, in mid June and July. Its markings vary and it may be darkish brown or tawny, with a black spot at the tip of the fore wing, sometimes with similar spots on the hind wings.

6 The Ringlet*
The Ringlet is sooty brown, with pale-ringed black spots of variable size, and sometimes white-centred. It likes shady lanes, and is found all over the British Isles.

* Like the butterflies on the following page, all these caterpillars feed on various grasses.

1 The Speckled Wood*

This dark brown butterfly has cream spots. Each fore wing-tip has a white-centred black eye-spot; the hind wings have 3 or 4 such spots. It is seen in shady lanes and the edges of woods, from May to October, in all parts of Britain.

2 The Wall Brown*

Seen all over Britain from May to September, this butterfly 'sunbathes', wings outstretched on warm walls. Orange-brown, with black markings, it has black eye-spots, white-centred, on its fore wings. The hind wing-spots vary in size and number.

3 The Marbled White*

This species is seen from mid-July to late August, in Midland and Southern England. Likes chalk and limestone soils. It is creamy-white, with black markings.

The caterpillars of all these 3 butterflies feed on grasses.

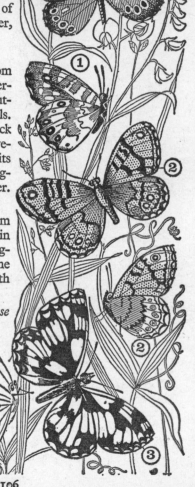

FRITILLARIES

Those shown here have golden-brown, black-veined upper wings and small front legs. Some hibernate in Winter.

1 The Pearl-bordered Fritillary

Common in wood-clearings, it is seen in May and June, and hibernates in Winter. The caterpillar feeds on Dog Violets.

The Small Pearl-bordered Fritillary (*not shown*)

Similar, but its hind-wing undersides have more silver spots. It emerges later (July to August).

2 The Queen of Spades Fritillary

A migrant butterfly, it arrives in May and stays until September. Large silver 'coin-like' patches stud the underside of its hind-wings.

The Dark Green Fritillary (*not shown*)

Common on moors and hillsides. Its underside has greenish hind-wings with iridescent spots. Natural food is Dog Violets.

3 The High Brown Fritillary

Widely distributed, but not North of Westmorland. Seen in early July to August. Underside light, with large silver discs.

4 The Silver-Washed Fritillary

Found in Southern England and Midland woods. Underside of hind wings matt green with silvery waves. Natural food: violets.

1 The Small Tortoiseshell

Common all over Britain, from May to October, in gardens and parks. It is orange-red, with yellow and black patches and with blue flecks on the edge of its hind wings. It lays its eggs on the Stinging Nettle.

2 The Peacock

Seen in most parts of this country from March until the late Autumn, when it hibernates. Its wings are velvety red-brown with large yellow, black and blue 'eyes'. Also lays its eggs on Stinging Nettles.

3 The Camberwell Beauty

This migrant butterfly is rare in Britain, seen in late Summer, mostly near the east coast. Its chocolate-brown wings bordered with black-speckled yellow, have blue spots just inside the brown. It lays its eggs on willow bushes.

4 The Comma

Fairly common, except in the North. Tawny brown and orange, black spotted, with 'comma' mark on the underside hind wing. Easy to recognise by ragged look at edges of wings. Again, its most common food is the Stinging Nettle.

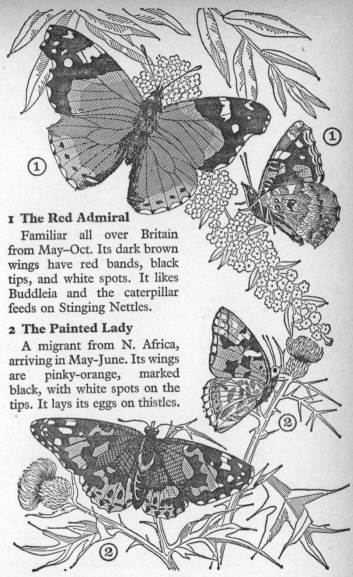

1 The Red Admiral

Familiar all over Britain from May–Oct. Its dark brown wings have red bands, black tips, and white spots. It likes Buddleia and the caterpillar feeds on Stinging Nettles.

2 The Painted Lady

A migrant from N. Africa, arriving in May-June. Its wings are pinky-orange, marked black, with white spots on the tips. It lays its eggs on thistles.

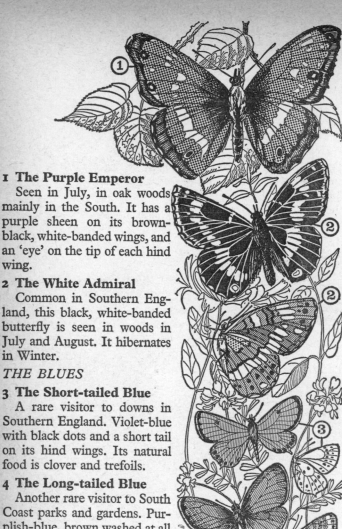

1 The Purple Emperor

Seen in July, in oak woods mainly in the South. It has a purple sheen on its brownblack, white-banded wings, and an 'eye' on the tip of each hind wing.

2 The White Admiral

Common in Southern England, this black, white-banded butterfly is seen in woods in July and August. It hibernates in Winter.

THE BLUES

3 The Short-tailed Blue

A rare visitor to downs in Southern England. Violet-blue with black dots and a short tail on its hind wings. Its natural food is clover and trefoils.

4 The Long-tailed Blue

Another rare visitor to South Coast parks and gardens. Purplish-blue, brown washed at all outer margins, it has two black spots and a slender black tail on its hind wings.

1 The Silver-studded Blue

From July to late August this butterfly is seen on sandy heaths in many areas. The male is violet-blue, the female dull brown. She lays her eggs on gorse, broom or heather.

2 The Brown Argus

Common in Southern counties, rarer in the North, this sooty-brown member of the 'blue' family lays its eggs on the plant of the Rock-rose, or Stork's-bill.

3 The Common Blue

Seen from May to September on heaths and meadows all over Britain. The male is mauve-blue with narrow black wing margins, the female brown, with orange-spots on wing edges. The eggs are laid on Bird's-foot Trefoil.

4 The Chalk Blue

One of the commonest 'blues' flying in late July and August on chalk downs in Southern England. The male is pale silver-blue with black wing borders and spots; the female is brown. They feed only on Horse-shoe Vetch.

5 The Small Blue

The smallest of the 'blues' haunting grassy hillsides of Southern England, from May to late June. It is blackish-blue. The caterpillars feed on Kidney Vetch.

1 The Small Copper

Common in open fields all over Britain, from early May to October. Fore-wings copper, with black margins and patches; hind-wings brown, with copper margins.

2 The Green Hairstreak

Named because of its green-coloured underside, its upper-side is brown. Common all over the country, flying from mid-May to June, in woods and meadows.

3 The Purple Hairstreak

Found in oak woods in all parts of Britain during July and August. The male is blackish purple; the female has two blue patches on the fore-wings.

4 The Swallow-tail

Our largest butterfly, now only seen in Norfolk. Its wings are yellow, marked with black and blue, with a round red patch at the lower inside corner of the hind wings. It appears in May and flies until August. Caterpillars feed on milk parsley.

THE WHITES

1 The Large White
Or the 'cabbage white', its caterpillars feed on this plant. Entirely black and white; seen in gardens May–October.

2 The Small White
Very like No. 1, but smaller and less black on wings. Hind wing underside is yellow and grey. Flies from May to October.

3 The Green-veined White
Called after its yellow-green 'green-veined' underside, its white wings have black tips and spots. Seen May–September.

4 The Orange Tip
Common. White, with orange wing-tips. Flies late April–June.

5 The Clouded Yellow
This butterfly's wings are orange, broadly edged in black and with black spot on the fore-wings, deep orange spot on hind-wings. Look for it in clover fields August–Sept.
The Pale Clouded Yellow is very like No. 5, but rarer and paler.

1 The Brimstone
The male is sulphur yellow, female greenish-white. Both have orange spots on each wing. Seen from March to October.

2 The Wood White
This fragile creamy-white butterfly has squarish black spots on its fore-wings. Flies from mid-May to August.

SKIPPERS

3 The Dingy Skipper
Small, active, early spring butterfly, seen on open chalky ground in Southern England.

4 The Grizzled Skipper
Seen all over England in May and June, on chalky downs. Black, with square white spots.

5 The Large Skipper
Tawny-yellow with markings of black. Flies from early June to mid-August.

6 The Small Skipper
Found in July to August in Southern England. Orange-brown with black margins and markings.

Some of our more rare butterflies to look for.
These butterflies can all be found in this country. Some in several districts, like the Duke of Burgundy Fritillary seen in Southern counties; some in one area only, like the Black-veined White, only found in Kent.

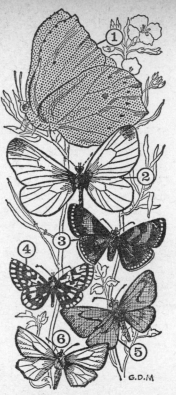

G.D.M

The Scotch Argus
The Marsh Fritillary
The Duke of Burgundy Fritillary
The Silver-studded Blue
The Adonis Blue
The Holly Blue
The Brown Hairstreak
The Black Hairstreak
The Chequered Skipper
The Essex Skipper
The Lulworth Skipper
The Black-veined White
The Mountain Ringlet

MOTHS YOU MAY SEE

There are 2,200 British moths,
– we can only show a very few
Usually they are divided into 2
kinds, 'macros', the big ones,
'micros' the small. We have,
however, shown a few moths,
(*life-size*) in each of 3 cate-
gories. (1) the Hawk moths,
(2) day-flying moths, and (3)
night-flying moths.

   Moths, like butterflies, have a complicated life-cycle. The
female lays eggs on one particular kind of plant, these hatch
into caterpillars, which, in turn, become chrysalides.

HAWK MOTHS

1 The Eyed Hawk Moth
Common from May to July in Southern England. Bark-brown
colour, with dark blue eye-like markings on pink hind-wings.
2 The Poplar Moth
Only seen near its food plants, – poplar sallow or willow. A
variable grey colour, with rust-red patches on the hind-wing.

1 The Puss Moth

This fairly common, fluffy grey-white moth flies from May to July. Its curious caterpillar is green with purple 'saddle'. Eats willow and poplar.

2 The Buff-Tip Moth

At rest this moth looks like a short broken twig. Fore-wings silver-grey, buff patch at the tip, hind-wings pale yellow-grey. Caterpillars seen grouped on leaves of willow, elm, lime, oak etc, in Autumn.

3 The Pale Tussock Moth

This greyish-white moth flies from April to June. Its green caterpillar has golden 'shaving-brush' tufts, and a red tail tuft. Likes beech trees.

4 The Peppered Moth

Named for its light, black-peppered wings imitating birch bark. Caterpillar (called a 'looper') moves in loops.

5 The Large Emerald

Largest of the 'Emeralds', common in birch and hazel woods in July–Aug. Wings pale green with white flecks.

6 The Drinker moth

Named thus because of the dew-drinking habit of its black hairy caterpillar. The moth is a chestnut brown. Marshy places in June to mid-August.

TIGER MOTHS are brightly coloured, with furry caterpillars.
1 The Garden Tiger, common in July and August in woods and gardens. Brown and white fore-wings, red hind wings.

DAY-FLYING MOTHS
Not all moths fly at night, and sometimes day-fliers are mistaken for butterflies.

2 The Orange-Underwing
Small moths, with brownish 'marbled' fore-wings, and orange bordered hind-wings. Caterpillars feed on birch trees.

3 The Cinnabar
This black and red moth is seen in meadows in June. Its caterpillar, striped black and orange, feeds on Rag-wort.

4 The Emperor Moth
Seen on waste-ground and moors in April and May. Fore-wings are brown-grey with large 'eye-spots', hind-wings orange.

5 The Magpie Moth
Black and white, with bands of yellow, and seen in May–June in gardens and woods. It feeds on gooseberry and red-currant.

6 The Vapour Moth
Males – golden brown with white wing spots. Females – no wings, look like long spiders.

BEETLES
of our countryside

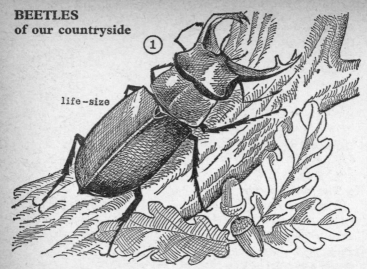

①

life-size

The scale beside each insect in this section shows its size.

Beetles belong to the Order of insects called Coleoptera, (meaning 'sheath wings'). There are nearly 4,000 species of these in Britain. They vary greatly in size and in habits, but they all have biting jaws and their front wings are tough, horny shields, called 'elytra'. The membrane-like hind wings are used for flying, but most beetles live on the ground, and many no longer have these flying wings. They eat a wide range of food, such as vegetable refuse, wood, woollens, fresh vegetables, fruit and animal matter. Their life-cycle is like that of the butterfly, with egg, larvae, pupa and adult stages – but in beetles the pupa stage is free, and not encased in a chrysalis.

1 The Stag Beetle

Our largest beetle, the male is over 3 ins. long, including its antler-like jaws (missing in the female). It lives and breeds in old tree-trunks, and feeds on the sap and juices of trees and plants. The wing cases are dark chestnut, and the antlers are blackish brown. The larvae can live from 3 to 12 years in mouldering wood, the adult beetle lives only 4 weeks.

1 The Cockchafer

A common beetle, seen in May on broad-leaved trees. Black body with grey hairs, brown wing cases, triangular white patches on sides. Lays eggs in batches on soil. Grub takes 4 years to develop.

2 The Tiger Beetle

This grass-green beetle is a fast mover, and sometimes flies. It has white markings on its wing case, and slender legs. Seen in sunny places in May.

3 The Dor Beetle

A squat blue-black beetle with finely ribbed wing cases. It lives on horse-dung. It makes a droning noise and swarms just after sunset.

4 The Bombardier Beetle

This beetle is named for its habit of squirting out acid which explodes on contact with air, and protects it from attack. Its compact, flat body is green or blue; antennae, legs, head and chest are rust-red.

5 The June Bug

Another 'chafer' beetle, seen in June-July. Body light brown, wing-case yellow with raised 'ribs'. Nocturnal, eats pine needles and deciduous trees.

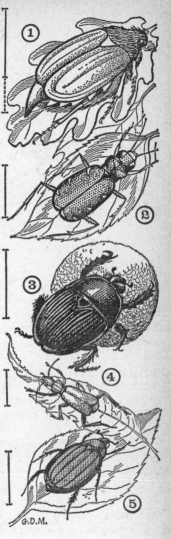

G.D.M.

119

1 The Colorado Beetle

Yellow, with long black stripes on its wing-case, and black spots on its base, it does much damage to potatoes. If you see this beetle, tell the police.

2 The 7-spot Ladybird

Known for the rhyme 'Ladybird, fly away home', this bright red beetle has 7 black spots. Its black thorax has 2 yellow patches. Gardeners like it because it eats aphids.

3 The Devil's Coach-horse

Seen in Summer, in woods and under moss, this completely black beetle, when attacked curls up the tip of its abdomen and throws out a nasty smell.

4 The Burying Beetle

An orange-red and black striped beetle, which feeds on dead animals. It digs round the carcass, which sinks into the ground, to provide food for the larvae.

5 The Glow Worm

The male is black-brown on top, yellowish underneath. Female, flightless, brown-grey maggot-shape and luminous. The male and larvae are luminous. Seen at night in woods in June and July.

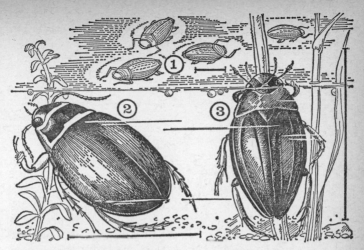

BEETLES THAT LIVE IN FRESH WATER

Many beetles live in fresh water. Some are 'surface beetles', others are completely aquatic. These aquatic beetles find their food, but cannot breathe, under water, so they store bubbles of air beneath their wing-cases, to take with them below. They have to surface regularly to renew their air supply.

1 Whirligig Beetles

A small, fast-moving surface beetle. Its glossy black body has elongated fore-legs. Seen on ponds in July and August.

2 The Great Diving Beetle

A ferocious beetle that preys on other aquatic life. It is dark brownish-green with yellow edges and yellow abdomen. Its flat hind legs have paddle-like bristles for swimming.

3 The Silver Water Beetle

One of our largest beetles, it is vegetarian and a slow swimmer. Its oval body is pitch-black with an olive sheen.

Some other beetles to look for

The Carrion Beetle	The Musk Beetle	The Bark Beetle
The Wasp Beetle	The Dung Beetle	The Click Beetle
The Carabid Beetle	The May Bug	The Leaf Beetle
The Oil Beetle	The Longhorn	

DRAGONFLIES AND DAMSELFLIES

These are among our most attractive insects. There are 2 groups, the large dragonflies which rest with wings open; and damselflies, which fold their wings above the body at rest. They have 4 wings, big eyes and very strong jaws. They both hunt other insects.

1 The Dragonfly

These restless, quick-flying insects live near water, where they lay their eggs. Their fierce-looking larvae, 1b, called nymphs live in ponds, where they catch worms with their extended 'masks'.

2 The Damselfly

Much more slender than the dragonflies, and smaller, with a very long metallic body.

3 The Mayfly

Common round inland ponds and lakes, these delicate long-tailed insects have a brief life as adults, often only a few hours, but the nymphs may take 3 years to develop.

1 The Stone Fly
These soft-bodied insects have brown wings, 2 long tails, and live near running water.

2 The Alder Fly
This stout little fly holds its wings above its black body when at rest among waterside plants, in early Summer.

3 The Pond Skater
These bugs have long, dark bodies, silvery underneath. They glide over pond surfaces on 4 very thin legs. They feed on other insects.

4 The Water Scorpion
This water bug creeps on the bottom of ponds. Its grey-brown body has a long breathing tube which pokes above the surface of the water.

5 The Caddis Fly
This small moth-like fly is famous because of its larva, which builds a portable home of shells, twigs etc., stuck to a silk web spun round its body.

123

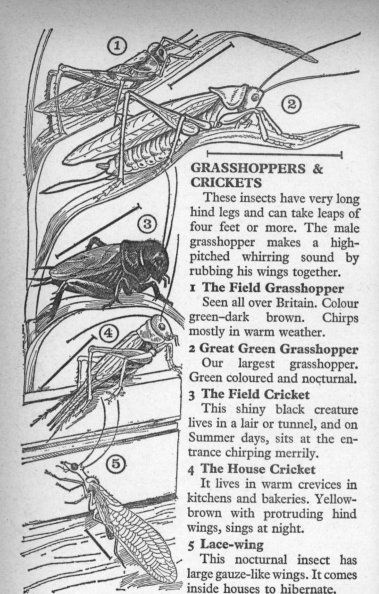

GRASSHOPPERS & CRICKETS

These insects have very long hind legs and can take leaps of four feet or more. The male grasshopper makes a high-pitched whirring sound by rubbing his wings together.

1 The Field Grasshopper

Seen all over Britain. Colour green–dark brown. Chirps mostly in warm weather.

2 Great Green Grasshopper

Our largest grasshopper. Green coloured and nocturnal.

3 The Field Cricket

This shiny black creature lives in a lair or tunnel, and on Summer days, sits at the entrance chirping merrily.

4 The House Cricket

It lives in warm crevices in kitchens and bakeries. Yellow-brown with protruding hind wings, sings at night.

5 Lace-wing

This nocturnal insect has large gauze-like wings. It comes inside houses to hibernate.

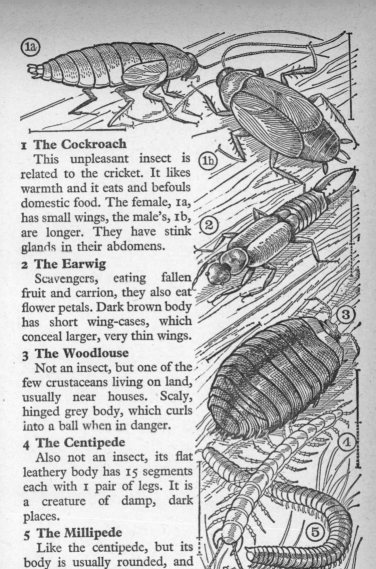

1 The Cockroach

This unpleasant insect is related to the cricket. It likes warmth and it eats and befouls domestic food. The female, 1a, has small wings, the male's, 1b, are longer. They have stink glands in their abdomens.

2 The Earwig

Scavengers, eating fallen fruit and carrion, they also eat flower petals. Dark brown body has short wing-cases, which conceal larger, very thin wings.

3 The Woodlouse

Not an insect, but one of the few crustaceans living on land, usually near houses. Scaly, hinged grey body, which curls into a ball when in danger.

4 The Centipede

Also not an insect, its flat leathery body has 15 segments each with 1 pair of legs. It is a creature of damp, dark places.

5 The Millipede

Like the centipede, but its body is usually rounded, and has 2 pairs of legs to each segment.

BEES AND WASPS

Many bees and wasps are 'social' insects, so named because they live together in nests, and help each other. There are over 250 different bees and 240 wasps in Britain – we can only show you the 4 best known species.

1 The Honey Bee

There are 3 kinds of bee in each nest or hive; (1a) drones or males, who do no work, (1b) workers who are the nurses of the hive, and (1c) the one Queen, who sometimes lays 1,000 eggs a day.

2 The Bumble Bee

This bee also has 3 'castes' in each nest, which they build in holes in the ground. They make a buzzing sound in flight, are larger than the honey-bee and black and yellow striped.

3 The Wasp

Related to bees, but with slimmer body, black, with yellow markings. They build nests from 'paper' which they make from old wood. They can sting several times – a bee can only sting once.

4 The Hornet

Our largest wasp, covered with brown hair, makes its nest with wood-pulp. Like all wasps its larvae eat small insects.

G.D.M.

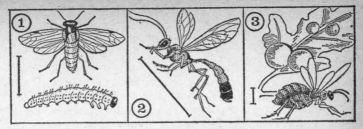

PARASITES OF THE HYMENOPTERA ORDER

There are many Wasps, Sawflies and Ichneumon flies in our countryside. They vary in size and habit – all are destructive. Sawflies are leaf-eaters. **1 The Gooseberry Sawfly** lays its eggs on the underside of gooseberry leaves. Ichneumon Flies are parasites, laying their eggs in caterpillars of other insects. **2 The Common Yellow Ophion** lays eggs on caterpillars of night moths. **3 The Gall Wasp** lays eggs and hatches larvae on trees and plants, which then form 'gall-tissue', e.g. oak-apples.

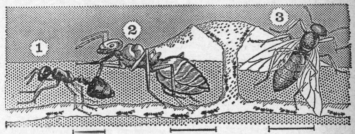

ANTS

Ants are social insects, living in thousands in ant-cities with a very complex social structure. As with bees, there are 3 kinds of ant in each 'city':— **1** the workers, **2** the egg-laying queens, and **3** the males. The workers look after the eggs and feed the young ants; the males do no work and immediately after mating they die. The queens live for many years, laying thousands of eggs, which become new independent colonies. The queen ant has wings when young; after mating and before she lays her eggs, she rubs off these wings. Ants develop through the same stages as beetles; first eggs, then larvae, then pupae.

MOLLUSCS

This group, the 2nd largest in the animal kingdom, includes snails, slugs, squids and mussels. Differing in appearance, they all have soft un-segmented bodies, and many have a shell or outer skeleton. The majority live in the sea.

GASTROPODS

This name means 'stomach-foot', and this largest class of molluscs includes all the land-living ones, and water-snails.

Order Pulmonata

1 The Great Grey Slug

One of our largest slugs, with a long, slim greyish body. Common in woods and gardens.

2 The Shelled Slug

This slug has a small shell at the thicker back end of its body. It feeds at night on worms.

3 The Large Black Slug

Seen in gardens and woods. A round-backed slug, usually jet black, sometimes white. It feeds on fungi. Life-span about 1 year.

G. D. M.

130

Up to 2½" high

Up to 1⅜" high

Up to ⅝" high

LAND SNAILS

Land snails have hollow coiled shells. From this shell the 'foot' emerges forming, in the front, the head with 2 pairs of tentacles; the longest pair has eyes at the tip. Land snails all breathe by a lung, eat fungi and decaying vegetation, and like damp, warm, rain.

Lung-breathing Snails

1 The Roman Snail

Common in gardens, it likes chalky soil. Its brown-yellow shell has 5 dark bands. Its body is slimy yellow-grey, rounded in front, pointed at the rear.

2 The Garden Snail

Smaller, with yellow, orange, or red-brown shell, often darkly banded. Seen in woods and gardens.

3 Round-mouthed Snail

Likes chalky soil. Colour varies from yellow to grey or dark flesh-colour, sometimes banded. Its coils are circular.

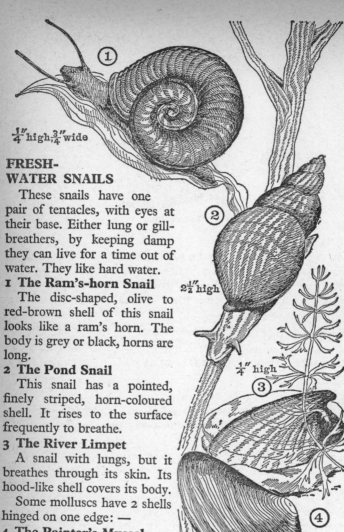

$\frac{1}{4}''$ high; $\frac{3}{4}''$ wide

② $2\frac{1}{2}''$ high

$\frac{1}{4}''$ high

Up to 4″long

FRESH-WATER SNAILS

These snails have one pair of tentacles, with eyes at their base. Either lung or gill-breathers, by keeping damp they can live for a time out of water. They like hard water.

1 The Ram's-horn Snail

The disc-shaped, olive to red-brown shell of this snail looks like a ram's horn. The body is grey or black, horns are long.

2 The Pond Snail

This snail has a pointed, finely striped, horn-coloured shell. It rises to the surface frequently to breathe.

3 The River Limpet

A snail with lungs, but it breathes through its skin. Its hood-like shell covers its body.

Some molluscs have 2 shells hinged on one edge: —

4 The Painter's Mussel

So called because formerly used as a palette by painters. Colour olive-yellow.

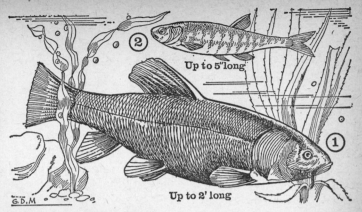

Up to 5" long

Up to 2' long

G.D.M

FRESH-WATER FISH

Many different kinds of fish are found in ponds, rivers, canals and lakes in Britain, some quite large, others small. Most of them can be eaten, though many have a muddy taste. Some only live in fast-running water, others like still lakes and ponds.

1 The Tench

A stocky fish, seen in slow-flowing water in South and East England. Slimy olive green with lighter, gold-shot sides, small scales and a barbel at each corner of its mouth.

2 The Minnow

A small, inquisitive fish, with olive-green back, striped silvery flanks and tiny scales. It lives in shoals, and is fast-moving. It needs clear, shallow, running water to live in.

3 The Pike

Large hunting fish, olive-green, with slanting stripes, long beak-like snout and big mouth and teeth. Lives 20–30 years.

Up to 3'6" long

133

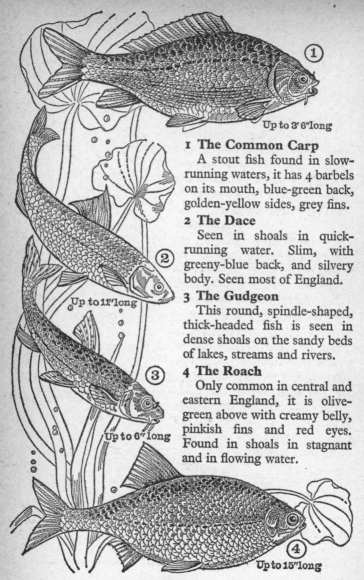

Up to 3'6"long

1 The Common Carp
A stout fish found in slow-running waters, it has 4 barbels on its mouth, blue-green back, golden-yellow sides, grey fins.

2 The Dace
Seen in shoals in quick-running water. Slim, with greeny-blue back, and silvery body. Seen most of England.

3 The Gudgeon
This round, spindle-shaped, thick-headed fish is seen in dense shoals on the sandy beds of lakes, streams and rivers.

4 The Roach
Only common in central and eastern England, it is olive-green above with creamy belly, pinkish fins and red eyes. Found in shoals in stagnant and in flowing water.

Up to 11"long

Up to 6"long

Up to 15"long

134

Up to 14" long

1 The Perch

This olive-green hunting fish has dark-banded flanks, two spiky, grey dorsal fins, and red belly fins. Lives in clear water and many are caught by anglers.

2 The Three-spined Stickleback

A lively little fish with interesting breeding habits. The male builds a nest, fertilises the eggs, and tends the young until they can be independent.

Up to 4" long

3 The Brown Trout

One of the three kinds of British Trout, it is found in mountain streams. Its colour varies with its surroundings.

Up to 18" long

4 The Bream

A large grey fish with a high back and flat sides, short back fin and long belly fin. It likes still deep waters.

Up to 20" long

eggs

alevin

The Salmon

The Salmon is one of the largest and most handsome fish in our rivers. It is a fish of northern countries, which leaves the Atlantic and travels to European rivers solely for the purpose of laying its eggs. It makes this dangerous journey, leaping over weirs and waterfalls, and travelling many miles upstream, between September and February.

The female or 'hen' fish looks for a clear, shallow gravel-bottomed place, where, with a flip of her tail, she makes a hollow nest, called a 'redd'. In this she lays up to 7,000 eggs which are then fertilised by the male, or 'cock'. She covers the eggs, and then they both travel back to the sea. About 100 days later the eggs hatch into tiny ½ in. long fish. They have a yolk sac attached to their bellies, on which they feed for 3 or 4 weeks until they are strong enough to be mobile.

When the salmon is about 4½ ins. long it is called a 'parr' and now it swims above the gravel surface. At this stage it is rainbow coloured. After a year or more in fresh-water is ready to go to sea, and its colour changes to silver; it vanishes for 18 months, before returning, once again to our rivers to breed.

When the salmon first reaches a river it is plump, storing as much nourishment as it can in its body. Once in fresh water it does not eat at all, so by the time it has spawned, and is ready to return to the sea, it is in very poor shape.

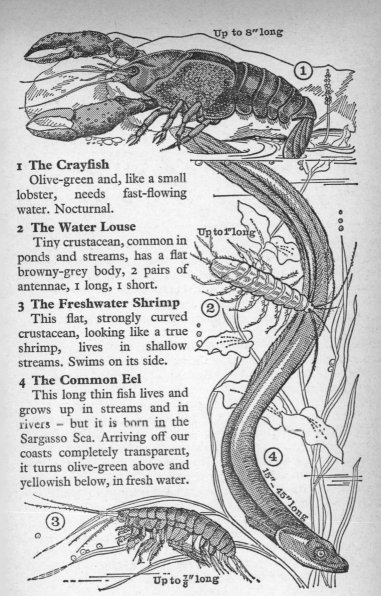

Up to 8″ long

1 The Crayfish
Olive-green and, like a small lobster, needs fast-flowing water. Nocturnal.

2 The Water Louse
Tiny crustacean, common in ponds and streams, has a flat browny-grey body, 2 pairs of antennae, 1 long, 1 short.

Up to 1″ long

3 The Freshwater Shrimp
This flat, strongly curved crustacean, looking like a true shrimp, lives in shallow streams. Swims on its side.

4 The Common Eel
This long thin fish lives and grows up in streams and in rivers – but it is born in the Sargasso Sea. Arriving off our coasts completely transparent, it turns olive-green above and yellowish below, in fresh water.

15″ – 45″ long

Up to $\frac{7}{8}$″ long

137

THE SEA-SHORE

This fascinating area lying between sea and land is home to hosts of creatures that have adapted themselves to this life of tides and storms. Some cling to rocks, others bury themselves in sand or mud, and some hide in the seaweeds. There are a great many – we can only show you a few.

You will find many shells, which are the protective covering of the molluscs, a group of backbone-less animals with soft bodies, who move by a muscular 'foot'. There are 4 classes of mollusc (1) The Polyplacophera or Chitons whose shell is made of movable plates, (2) The Gastropods, or univalves, with shells in one piece, (3) The Bi-valves, with 2 hinged shells, and (4) The Cephalods, with shells hidden, like the Octopus.

On these 2 pages there are 19 different kinds of shell that you may find. Can you see to which of the four classes they belong.

1 *The Common Periwinkle*
2 *The Flat Periwinkle*
3 *The Painted Top Shell*
4 *The Barnacle*
5 *The Common Dog Whelk*
6 *The Common Cockle*
7 *The Limpet*
8 *The Common Whelk*
9 *The Cowrie*
10 *The Sand Gaper*
11 *The Mussel*
12 *The Warty Venus*
13 *The Striped Venus*
14 **and** 15 *Tellins*
16 *The Netted Dog Whelk*
17 *The Razor Shell*
18 *The Chiton*
19 *The Elephant Tusk*

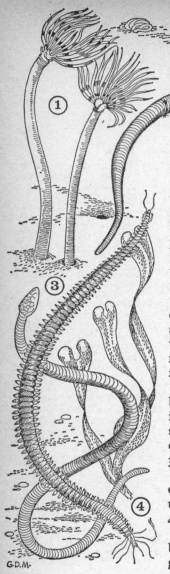

SHORE WORMS

Many shore creatures live under the sandy surface of the beach. You see their breathing tubes or holes appearing above the sand. Sometimes, in shallow pools, you see the stiff brush-like crown of tentacles pushing their way out of the 'chimneys' as the worm comes up for air.

1 The Peacock Worm

Up to 12 ins. long, but with only 4 ins. of tube visible above the mud, this beautiful worm has a crown of white, red-tipped, plumes.

2 The Lug Worm

A very common worm, used by fishermen for bait. 10–12 ins. long, dark brown, its U-shaped burrow has a pile of castings at the end.

3 The Rag Worm

About 4 ins. long, red, green, or yellow, this worm hides under rocks and stones.

4 The Red-line Worm

Up to 6 ins. long and reddish brown, this worm lives in gravel under rocks and seaweed.

STARFISH

These spiny animals cannot live out of water. They feed on shellfish.

1 The Cushion Starfish

4 ins. found mostly on the S. Coast, under stones.

2 The Common Starfish

Common on all our coasts, about 6 ins. across (can grow to 20 ins.) with 5 radiating arms, each with 2 rows of 'tube-feet' underneath. Colour yellowish-red.

3 The Brittle Starfish

This 12 ins. animal of the low-shore, has 5 long, thin, easily-broken arms, which it can renew.

SEA URCHINS

Cousins of the starfish, these creatures have a round chalky shell, or test, covered with long movable spines.

4 The Common Sea-Urchin

About 2 ins. across, purple in colour, with very long spines.

5 The Purple-Heart Urchin

Domed on top, flat underneath, it lives in groups in sand at low-tide mark.

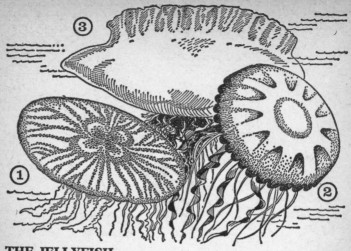

THE JELLYFISH

These strange creatures are almost entirely composed of water, so, if stranded by the tide, soon dry up and die. They swim by opening and closing their parachute-like bodies. The long, hanging tentacles contain stinging cells which are used to ensnare and paralyse small fish and other creatures.

1 The White Jellyfish

Our most common jellyfish, up to 1 ft. across, whitish, with 4 pale mauve crescents on its underside.

2 The Compass Jellyfish

This beautiful pale yellow jellyfish, 8 ins. across, has brown markings and 4 long brown tentacles which can sting severely.

3 The Portuguese Man of War

This dangerous Mediterranean creature, blown to our South coasts, has a 6 in. gas-filled blue float, and tentacles several feet long with powerful and deadly stings.

SEA-ANEMONES

These flower-like animals catch food with swaying tentacles.

4 The Dahlia Anemone

5 The Snake-locks Anemone

142

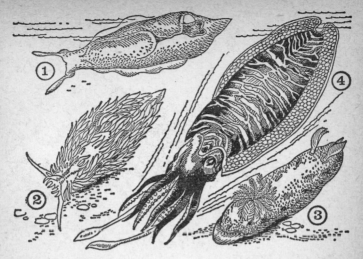

GASTROPODS

You have already met the creatures with a shell big enough to cover the body. The similar Sea-slugs are animals whose shell is very small or non-existent.

1 The Sea-Hare

The largest of our sea-slugs, up to 6 ins. long, reddish-brown or olive green, it feeds on the sea-lettuce.

2 The Grey Sea-slug

A widely distributed slug, feeding on sea-anemones. It is up to 3 ins. long, with a fur-like covering to its body.

3 The Sea Lemon

This animal, 2 ins. long, resembles the sponges on which it feeds. Yellow-pink, green or brown blotched, it has a 'plume' of gills at one end, 2 pairs of feathery tentacles at the other.

THE CUTTLEFISH

This creature's shell, a chalky oval object found on beaches, is embedded in its body, 2 large black eyes, a parrot-like beak, 8 arms growing out of its head, and 2 long tentacles used to catch its prey. When disturbed it ejects a stream of inky liquid, called 'sepia', as a smoke-screen.

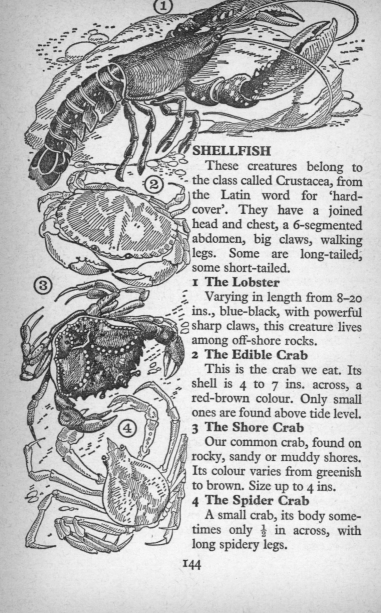

SHELLFISH

These creatures belong to the class called Crustacea, from the Latin word for 'hard-cover'. They have a joined head and chest, a 6-segmented abdomen, big claws, walking legs. Some are long-tailed, some short-tailed.

1 The Lobster

Varying in length from 8–20 ins., blue-black, with powerful sharp claws, this creature lives among off-shore rocks.

2 The Edible Crab

This is the crab we eat. Its shell is 4 to 7 ins. across, a red-brown colour. Only small ones are found above tide level.

3 The Shore Crab

Our common crab, found on rocky, sandy or muddy shores. Its colour varies from greenish to brown. Size up to 4 ins.

4 The Spider Crab

A small crab, its body sometimes only $\frac{1}{2}$ in across, with long spidery legs.

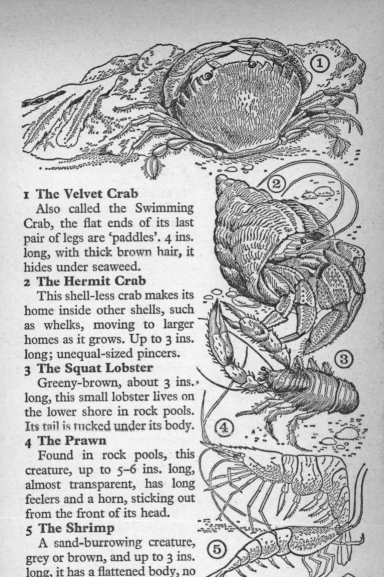

1 The Velvet Crab

Also called the Swimming Crab, the flat ends of its last pair of legs are 'paddles'. 4 ins. long, with thick brown hair, it hides under seaweed.

2 The Hermit Crab

This shell-less crab makes its home inside other shells, such as whelks, moving to larger homes as it grows. Up to 3 ins. long; unequal-sized pincers.

3 The Squat Lobster

Greeny-brown, about 3 ins. long, this small lobster lives on the lower shore in rock pools. Its tail is tucked under its body.

4 The Prawn

Found in rock pools, this creature, up to 5–6 ins. long, almost transparent, has long feelers and a horn, sticking out from the front of its head.

5 The Shrimp

A sand-burrowing creature, grey or brown, and up to 3 ins. long, it has a flattened body, no horn and burrows by day.

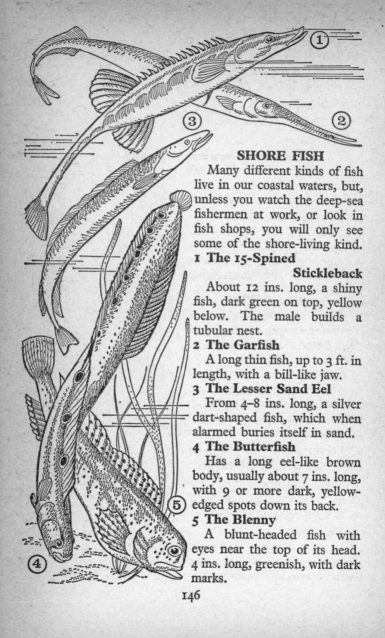

SHORE FISH

Many different kinds of fish live in our coastal waters, but, unless you watch the deep-sea fishermen at work, or look in fish shops, you will only see some of the shore-living kind.

1 The 15-Spined Stickleback

About 12 ins. long, a shiny fish, dark green on top, yellow below. The male builds a tubular nest.

2 The Garfish

A long thin fish, up to 3 ft. in length, with a bill-like jaw.

3 The Lesser Sand Eel

From 4–8 ins. long, a silver dart-shaped fish, which when alarmed buries itself in sand.

4 The Butterfish

Has a long eel-like brown body, usually about 7 ins. long, with 9 or more dark, yellow-edged spots down its back.

5 The Blenny

A blunt-headed fish with eyes near the top of its head. 4 ins. long, greenish, with dark marks.

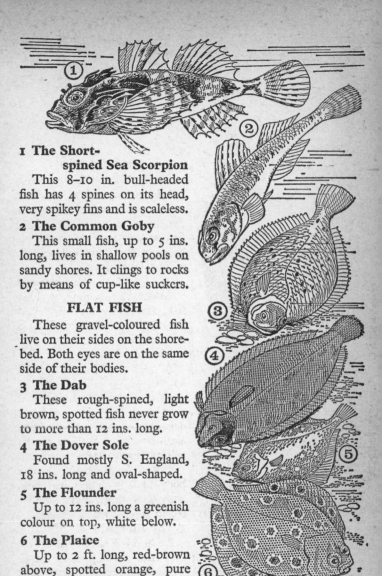

1 The Short-
spined Sea Scorpion
This 8–10 in. bull-headed fish has 4 spines on its head, very spikey fins and is scaleless.

2 The Common Goby
This small fish, up to 5 ins. long, lives in shallow pools on sandy shores. It clings to rocks by means of cup-like suckers.

FLAT FISH
These gravel-coloured fish live on their sides on the shore-bed. Both eyes are on the same side of their bodies.

3 The Dab
These rough-spined, light brown, spotted fish never grow to more than 12 ins. long.

4 The Dover Sole
Found mostly S. England, 18 ins. long and oval-shaped.

5 The Flounder
Up to 12 ins. long a greenish colour on top, white below.

6 The Plaice
Up to 2 ft. long, red-brown above, spotted orange, pure white below, and smooth.

G.D.N.

147

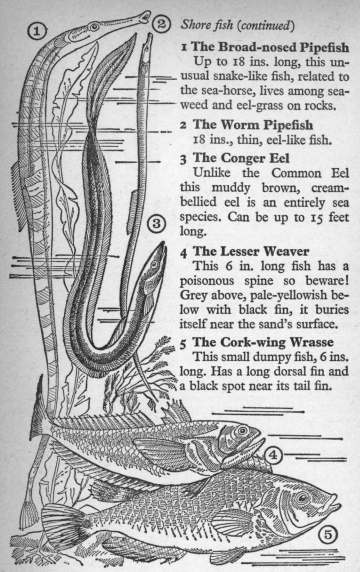

1 The Broad-nosed Pipefish
Up to 18 ins. long, this unusual snake-like fish, related to the sea-horse, lives among seaweed and eel-grass on rocks.

2 The Worm Pipefish
18 ins., thin, eel-like fish.

3 The Conger Eel
Unlike the Common Eel this muddy brown, cream-bellied eel is an entirely sea species. Can be up to 15 feet long.

4 The Lesser Weaver
This 6 in. long fish has a poisonous spine so beware! Grey above, pale-yellowish below with black fin, it buries itself near the sand's surface.

5 The Cork-wing Wrasse
This small dumpy fish, 6 ins. long. Has a long dorsal fin and a black spot near its tail fin.

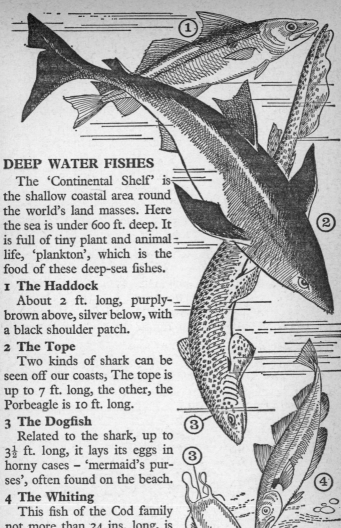

DEEP WATER FISHES

The 'Continental Shelf' is the shallow coastal area round the world's land masses. Here the sea is under 600 ft. deep. It is full of tiny plant and animal life, 'plankton', which is the food of these deep-sea fishes.

1 The Haddock

About 2 ft. long, purply-brown above, silver below, with a black shoulder patch.

2 The Tope

Two kinds of shark can be seen off our coasts, The tope is up to 7 ft. long, the other, the Porbeagle is 10 ft. long.

3 The Dogfish

Related to the shark, up to $3\frac{1}{2}$ ft. long, it lays its eggs in horny cases – 'mermaid's purses', often found on the beach.

4 The Whiting

This fish of the Cod family not more than 24 ins. long, is muddy green above, silvery below, it has a black spot by its pectoral fin.

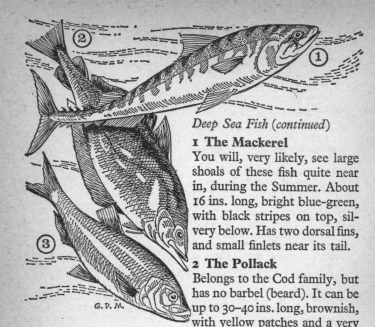

Deep Sea Fish (continued)

1 The Mackerel

You will, very likely, see large shoals of these fish quite near in, during the Summer. About 16 ins. long, bright blue-green, with black stripes on top, silvery below. Has two dorsal fins, and small finlets near its tail.

2 The Pollack

Belongs to the Cod family, but has no barbel (beard). It can be up to 30–40 ins. long, brownish, with yellow patches and a very protruding lower jaw.

3 The Herring

Our best-known and commercially most important deep-sea fish. It grows up to 1 ft., is silvery colour, and covered with scales. It has only one dorsal fin and, unlike most other fish, it has no line running from head to tail. It feeds on plankton and moves in enormous shoals in its search for this food. It is eaten fresh, and also smoked, as kippers and bloaters.

★　　★　　★

These pages about the creatures who live on our beaches and in our off-shore waters, and those that are caught further out on the Continental Shelf, are necessarily very few. There are so many thousands of fascinating animals and interesting fishes around our coasts that to tell you about them, even briefly, would need many more pages than there are in this whole book. Your library will be able to give you the names of some of the many books that specialise in these subjects.

Words Used
in this Book

abandoned, given up or left empty.

abdomen, the lower stomach or belly.

adapt (to), adapted, to change, or having changed, one's own habits and needs so as to fit in with the surrounding climate or countryside.

agile, nimble. Able to move about quickly and easily.

alarmed, frightened or scared.

alight, to 'land' from flight in the air.

allies, friends or same kinds of creatures.

amphibians, creatures which live both on land and in the water. (See page 37.)

ancestors, one's grandparents and their relations stretching back into the past.

antennae, the two feelers on the head of an insect, used to feel objects in front of them.

antler, the horn of a stag or deer with offshoots, shaped like the branches of a tree.

aphids, tiny insects which feed on plants.

aquatic, living on or under the water.

associated with, joined to or connected with something.

barbel, a piece hanging down from the lower lip of a fish, like a beard.

barren, land on which crops will not grow.

beak shield, a small piece in front of the beak to shield it from harm.

befouls, makes dirty.

Birdsfoot trefoil, small yellow flowers, leaves with three leaflets, seed cases arranged like a bird's foot. (Shown on page 111, the little flower next to No. 3.)

black-peppered, covered in little black spots.

Buddleia, garden bush with long sprays of sweet-smelling mauve or white flowers. (Shown at top of page 109.)

buff – buffish, dull yellowish colour.

camouflaged, made up of a colour or different colours so as to look the same as the nearby surroundings.

canine teeth, strong pointed teeth.

carcass, the body of a dead creature.

castes, kinds of the same type of creatures which are different because of the work they do. For instance, amongst ants and bees, there are the workers, the drones and the queens.

castings, a little pile of earth or sand the same shape as a worm and pushed out as he moves along.

cavities, hollow places, holes.

characteristic song, the song which is special to one kind of bird (e.g. 'cuckoo').

chrysalis, the stage of a butterfly or other insect between caterpillar and the fully grown creature. The caterpillar spins a silky case and goes into a kind of sleep until it is ready to come out again as a butterfly.

cocoon, a silky case spun by the larva of an insect to protect it when it becomes a chrysalis.

colonies, colony, in this book a colony means a group of creatures of the same kind living all together, but away from other creatures.

commercially, trading to make money.

compact, closely or neatly packed together.

complex, mixed together with lots of different ways of doing things.

composed of, made up of.

conifer, coniferous, a tree or bush which has cones such as a fir tree.

Continental Shelf, under the sea all around the Continent of Europe the sea bed is made up of a 'shelf' which is not so deep as the sea-bed of the surrounding Atlantic Ocean.

courtship display, the show which a creature (usually a bird) puts on to attract a mate.

crescent, the shape of the young moon.

crest, a piece growing out of the top of a bird's head, usually made up of feathers.

crown, top of the head.

crustacean, a creature having a hard cover or shell.

deciduous, a term used to describe trees which lose their leaves in the Autumn and grow them again in the Spring.

distinguishing feature, that special thing which makes a

creature different from those all around it.

distributed (widely), found in most parts.

dorsal fin, the fin on or near the back of a fish.

drab, drabber, made up of dull colours.

ear covert, the covering over a creature's ear-hole.

eject, to push out.

elaborate, worked out with great care and having a lot of detail.

elongated, made longer, or stretched out. Something which is much longer than it is wide.

elusive, difficult to find because it keeps out of the way.

ensnare (to), to trap.

environment, a creature's surroundings, the countryside around.

erected, made to stand upright.

evidence, signs of.

extensive, large or far-reaching.

external, on the outside.

facial, on the face.

flanks, sides.

flexible, able to bend without breaking.

foliage, a collection of leaves growing on a plant.

forage for (to), to search for food or anything else needed for life.

fore legs, front legs.

fragile, dainty, easily broken.

frequenting, going often to a place.

fungi, soft, spongy plants like toadstools.

gills, the small parts through which a fish 'breathes' water.

glossy, shiny.

graduated, getting smaller (or larger) bit by bit.

granaries, where corn is stored.

habitat, place in which something lives, its home.

haunt, a place where a creature usually lives or visits.

haunting, visiting a particular area or type of area, often.

heritage, something which belongs to you because it has been handed down from one's parents or ancestors.

hibernate, to go into a warm safe place for the Winter, or to go to sleep during the Winter.

hind, at the back. For instance the hind legs are the back legs.

Horseshoe Vetch, like a very tiny pea plant (shown by No. 4 on page 111).

hosts, (1) a quantity of creatures of all the same kind living together, or (2) creatures which have other smaller creatures living on them.

human habitations, houses, homes or other places where people live.

immigrate, to travel to this country from other lands.

inaccessible, cannot be got at, cannot be reached.

incisor, one of the front or cutting teeth.

inconspicuous, not easily noticed.

inhabitant, a creature which lives in a particular place or home.

inquisitive, wanting to know what is going on all around, i.e. 'nosey'.

internal organs, the parts inside a creature, e.g. the heart, the stomach, etc.

invertebrates, creatures which do not have a spine or back bone.

investigate, try to find out what is going on.

iridescent, showing colours like those of the rainbow, changing colour when moving.

larva, a caterpillar or grub, – the stage of an insect between leaving the egg and forming into a chrysalis.

leaf-nosed, nose shaped like a leaf.

lichen, moss-like plant.

life cycle, the stages of life which a creature goes through from birth to death.

lilting, sweet singing with marked swing.

lobed, having lobes or little fleshy bits sticking out or hanging down. For instance, the small bits hanging down at the bottom of your ears are called lobes.

location (echo), finding out the exact place of something through the echo of a sound.

luminous, something which gives out a little light at night.

lyre-shaped, shaped like a lyre (see tail of bird No. 2 on page 100).

mammals, class of animals who suckle their young (see page 7).

mammary, milk producing.

margins, the edges of.

marine, in or belonging to the sea.

melodious, a tuneful or pretty sound or noise.

membranes, a bendable connecting tissue or lining in an animal or plant body.

metallic, looking like metal.

migrant, a creature which migrates. See migrate.

migrate, to journey from one country to the other in search of food, better weather, for breeding or for some other reason.

mimic, copy the sounds of or act like someone else.

monotonous, sameness of tone or note, dull with no change or variety.

mottled, covered in spots or blotches.

mouldering, decaying or rotting.

moustachial, like a moustache.

muzzle, the part of an animal's face which includes the nose and mouth.

nape, back of the neck.

native, a creature which lives in the area where it was born or reared.

nocturnal, a creature which sleeps during the day and is active at night.

nymphs, larvae of the dragonfly or damselfly families.

ochre-coloured, pale brownish yellow.

orb-web, a round web.

palette, the board on which a painter keeps or mixes his paint.

palmate antlers, antlers on a deer which are shaped like a hand (see page 30).

paralyse (to), to make powerless or unable to move.

parasites, parasitic, plant or animal that grows on another, feeding from it.

parotid, in front of the ear.

passage visitor, bird of passage, a bird, which does not live all the time in Great Britain, but stops off here on its way between one country and another.

pectoral fin, breast-fin of fish.

piratical, like a pirate, or stealing from other creatures by force.

plankton, very tiny forms of life found in sea, rivers and lakes which fish feed on (see page 149).

plumage, a bird's feathers.

portable, something you can carry around with you.

primary feathers, the feathers on the edges of a bird's wings.

profile, the view of a creature (or person) seen from one side only.

projecting, sticking out.

protruding, sticking out.

pupa, the same as a chrysalis (see page 103).

radiating arms, arms which stretch in all directions.

ragwort, a large tall course weed with lots of small yellow daisy-like flowers bunched at the top.

remote, quiet, where few people go.

resident, a creature living in a particular area or country.

resourceful, able to use its head to find a way out of a difficulty. Or to find a way of supplying something it needs.

rigid, stiff or still.

rodents, a gnawing animal like a mouse or rat.

rudder, broad flat wooden piece on a boat used in steering.

rump, behind or lower end of backbone.

russet, rusty or reddish-brown.

scale, the way in which something large is drawn smaller to a set amount. For instance, with some maps, a mile on the ground is shown by an inch on the map.

secretion, secretary, storing up fluid.

secretive, shy and keeping away from other creatures, especially from man.

segments, bits which joined together make up the whole thing. Sections.

seldom, hardly ever, not often.

selective, choosey, picks out the best.

sheen, shiny surface which catches the light.

shoal, a great number of fish swimming around all together.

shy, easily startled, timid, keeping out of sight of humans.

skeleton, outside or inside framework of bones or shell.

skulk, skulking, to keep or keeping out of the way or hiding from other creatures, especially from man.

sociable, friendly, willing to live near or with other creatures.

social, living together in groups and keeping one another.

social structure, the way of life of a type of creature.

solitary, living alone. A creature living by itself, with perhaps the company of its mate and babies, but keeping away from others.

species, a particular kind of creature. For instance, man is a species of animal.

spined, having spines or sharp ridges sticking out.

spirally, winding round and round and also moving upwards or downwards at the same time, like the thread of a screw or some staircases.

squat, a shape of almost the same width, breadth and height. Chunky.

stagnant water, water which is still and cannot run away. Usually becomes dirty and smelly.

stork's-bill, like a small geranium with purple flowers – when they fall the seed pod looks just like a stork's bill.

streamlined, made in a smooth shape so as to give the least resistance to air or water. For instance, an aeroplane (or a paper dart) are made so that there are no bits sticking out.

sturdier, more sturdy or more strongly built.

subdued colour, a greyish or not very bright colour.

suburban, living near or on the outskirts of a big town.

sulphur yellow, a pale yellow.

surface, the outside or (for water) the top.

swarm, (to), to gather all together in large numbers. Used mostly to describe insects doing this.

symmetrical, beautiful because all the parts are even shaped.

tawny, a yellowish brown.

tentacles, feelers or long slender 'arms' of a wild creature used for finding out which things are nearby or used for getting about.

thorax, the part of an animal's body between the neck and the stomach.

transparent, something you can see through.

trefoils, plants with leaves made up of three leaflets like clover.

triangular, a shape having three sides and three angles or corners.

tubular, like a tube, i.e. long and hollow.

ungainly, clumsy or awkward.

unsegmented, a continuous shape, not divided into parts. For instance, the 'quarters' of an orange are really segments, So a peeled orange being made up of segments is segmented, but a rubber ball is unsegmented.

variable, likely to change.

vegetarian, a creature which only eats vegetable matter, grass and berries, and does not eat meat.

venomous, having a poisonous bite or sting. This word is usually used in connection with dangerous snakes.

ventilator shafts, little tunnels from below ground which go up to the surface, to let in fresh air.

vertebrates, creatures which have a series of bones from head to tail (or where the tail would be) known as a backbone or spine.

vertical, pointing (or standing) upright.

vocal, making a lot of noise with the beak or mouth.

waders, wading, creatures which walk about in water, mud or wet sand.

warble, sing in gentle continuous trilling manner.

wattle, the fleshy part above the head or below the throat of a turkey or similar bird.

webbed, having webs or stretches of skin joining up the toes in a bird or in a bat, joining the bones of the wings to the body.

weevil, kind of beetle, which feeds on grain, nuts, fruit and leaves.

wedge-shaped, like a wedge. Thicker at one end than at the other. Many packs of cheese are wedge-shaped.

INDEX TO WILD CREATURES

The publishers of this book hope you have found it enjoyable. It is one of a series of pocket-money-price paperbacks. Specially designed for young people. If you care to write to us at the address on page 3, we shall be delighted to hear from you and will gladly send you a copy of our current catalogue.